Strawberry Cheesecake *(recipe, pages 178 and 179)*

Mushroom Kabobs *(recipe, page 140)*

# Weight Watchers.

*Light & Easy*

## COOKBOOK

Oxmoor House.

Library of Congress Catalog Card Number: 97-65132
ISBN: 0-8487-1626-4

Manufactured in the United States of America
Second Printing 1997

Be sure to check with your health-care provider before making any changes in your diet.

*Weight Watchers* is a registered trademark of Weight Watchers International, Inc., and is used under license by Healthy Living, Inc.

Editor-in-Chief: Nancy Fitzpatrick Wyatt
Senior Foods Editor: Katherine M. Eakin
Senior Editor, Editorial Services: Olivia Kindig Wells
Art Director: James Boone

*Weight Watchers Light & Easy Cookbook*

Editor: Deborah Garrison Lowery
Assistant Foods Editor: Kathryn Matuszak, R.D.
Associate Art Director: Cynthia R. Cooper
Designer: Clare T. Minges
Editorial Coordinator: Kay Hicks
Editorial Assistants: Valorie J. Cooper, Leslie Katherine Monk
Proofreaders: Catherine S. Ritter, Kathryn Stroud
Indexer: Jacqueline Giovanelli
Director, Test Kitchens: Kathleen Royal Phillips
Assistant Director, Test Kitchens: Gayle Hays Sadler
Test Kitchens Home Economists: Susan Hall Bellows, Julie Christopher, Michele Brown Fuller, Natalie E. King, Elizabeth Tyler Luckett, Jan Moon, Iris Crawley O'Brien, Jan A. Smith
Senior Photographer: Jim Bathie
Photographer: Tina Evans
Senior Photo Stylist: Kay E. Clarke
Photo Stylist: Virginia Cravens
Publishing Systems Administrator: Rick Tucker
Production and Distribution Director: Phillip Lee
Associate Production Manager: Vanessa Cobbs Richardson

**We're Here For You!**

We at Oxmoor House are dedicated to serving you with reliable information that expands your imagination and enriches your life. We welcome your comments and suggestions. Please write us at:

Oxmoor House, Inc.
Editor, *Weight Watchers Light & Easy Cookbook*
2100 Lakeshore Drive
Birmingham, AL 35209

To order additional publications, call 1-205-877-6560.

*Cover:* Southwestern Chicken Pasta, page 93
*Back Cover:* Peach Crumble, page 170
Photography by Jim Bathie; styling by Kay E. Clarke

# Contents

# Steps to a Light & Easy Lifestyle

You'll love the way we've made life simpler, especially if you're trying to lose pounds or to maintain your weight. Recipes in this book are the first to use the guidelines for The Freedom Plan, which is based on steps that have made Weight Watchers and its followers successful:

1. Eat fewer calories than you're eating now.
2. Increase your activity level to burn more calories.
3. Develop a strong motivation to change your own behaviors and strategies for losing weight.
4. Join a support group to reinforce, guide, and encourage your efforts.

## Use This Book to Make Life Easier

The way we've organized this cookbook, particularly the recipe pages, you'll find it a snap to follow any eating plan—whether you're simply counting fat grams or calories, or following The Freedom Plan or Fat & Fiber Plan from Weight Watchers. To make your life easier, we've included the following useful information:

### For Your Health:

• A complete nutrient analysis of each serving with every recipe.
• Selections for Protein/Milk, Bread, Fruit/Vegetable, Fat, and Optional Calories to use with any eating plan that calls for counting selections or exchanges.
• A low-fat substitution chart on page 188.

### For Your Convenience:

• Easy recipe directions presented in a numbered step-by-step format.
• Over 100 tips for quicker, easier cooking on the recipe pages where you need them.
• A bonus list of 20 super-quick recipes. You'll find a listing and page reference for 15-Minute Recipes in the index on page 192.

### Our Best-Kept Weight Loss Secrets

• Choose foods that require lots of chewing like fresh fruit and whole grain breads.
• Sip a hot or cold low-calorie beverage instead of snacking.
• Don't give up your favorite formerly forbidden foods (no kidding!). Instead, eat lightly and skip snacks on the days you decide to indulge.
• Keep a food diary and note when, where, and how much you eat. Once you know your eating triggers, you can avoid them or find non-food ways to comfort yourself.
• Make exercise a routine activity. Exercising on a regular basis is more important than the type of activity you do.
• Eat slowly and you'll eat less.

# How to Use Our Recipes

Need to know how long it takes to prepare each recipe? Want nutrient or Selection values per serving? All are at your fingertips; see the sample recipe below.

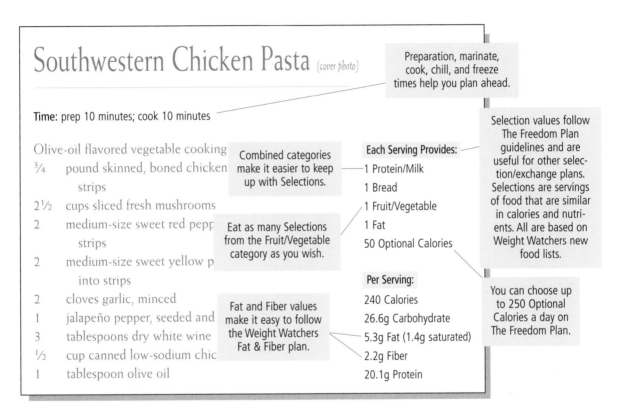

## Southwestern Chicken Pasta *(cover photo)*

**Time:** prep 10 minutes; cook 10 minutes

Olive-oil flavored vegetable cooking
¾    pound skinned, boned chicken
        strips
2½   cups sliced fresh mushrooms
2     medium-size sweet red pepp
        strips
2     medium-size sweet yellow p
        into strips
2     cloves garlic, minced
1     jalapeño pepper, seeded and
3     tablespoons dry white wine
½    cup canned low-sodium chic
1     tablespoon olive oil

Preparation, marinate, cook, chill, and freeze times help you plan ahead.

Combined categories make it easier to keep up with Selections.

Eat as many Selections from the Fruit/Vegetable category as you wish.

Fat and Fiber values make it easy to follow the Weight Watchers Fat & Fiber plan.

**Each Serving Provides:**
1 Protein/Milk
1 Bread
1 Fruit/Vegetable
1 Fat
50 Optional Calories

**Per Serving:**
240 Calories
26.6g Carbohydrate
5.3g Fat (1.4g saturated)
2.2g Fiber
20.1g Protein

Selection values follow The Freedom Plan guidelines and are useful for other selection/exchange plans. Selections are servings of food that are similar in calories and nutrients. All are based on Weight Watchers new food lists.

You can choose up to 250 Optional Calories a day on The Freedom Plan.

## The New Freedom Plan; Here's How It Works

Now you can control what you eat, rather than letting your diet control you. Use the new food and activity plans on page 8. You'll notice these changes:

• Portion sizes are more realistic.
• No more weighing your food! You can throw away the scales when you follow the Selection system listed in the chart at the top of page 8.
• Food categories have been simplified to make counting Selections simpler. Instead of keeping

tabs on the number of Selections from both Protein and Milk categories, the two have been combined into a single category.
• As always, Selections from the Fruit/Vegetable category are unlimited, and extra helpings do not count as Optional Calories.

| The Freedom Plan Daily Food Guide For Women | | | |
|---|---|---|---|
| FOOD CATEGORY | NUMBER OF FOOD SELECTIONS FOR YOUR WEIGHT | | |
| | Less than 175 pounds | 175 to 250 pounds | Over 250 pounds |
| Protein/Milk | 5-6 | 6-7 | 7-8 |
| Bread | 4-5 | 6-7 | 8-9 |
| Fruit/Vegetable | 5 or more | 5 or more | 5 or more |
| Fat | 2-3 | 3-4 | 4-5 |
| Glasses of Water | 6 or more | 6 or more | 6 or more |
| Optional Calories | up to 250 | up to 250 | up to 250 |

© Weight Watchers International

# Don't Forget Fitness for a Balanced Life

A vital part of The Freedom Plan from Weight Watchers includes regular physical activity. Use the following definitions to help you use the activity chart below:

**Fat Burner Selection**: 10 minutes of a moderately intense activity that uses large muscles in a rhythmic, repetitive way, such as walking, swimming, biking, dancing, climbing stairs, or doing yard work.
**Lean Builder Selection**: 20 repetitions of an activity that tones and firms your muscles, such as wall presses, leg lifts, heel raisers, or arm curls.
**Stretch Selection**: Holding a particular stretch position for up to 30 seconds, then repeating the stretch 3 to 5 times. Includes hamstring stretch, calf stretch, shoulder stretch, and chest stretch.

| The Freedom Plan Daily Activity Guide | | | |
|---|---|---|---|
| ACTIVITY | NUMBER OF ACTIVITY SELECTIONS FOR YOUR WEIGHT | | |
| | Less than 175 pounds | 175 to 250 pounds | over 250 pounds |
| Fat Burners | 2-3 | 2-3 | 2-3 |
| Lean Builders | 1 or more | 1 or more | 1 or more |
| Stretches | 1 or more | 1 or more | 1 or more |

© Weight Watchers International

# breads

# Whole Wheat Apple Pancakes

**Time:** prep 15 minutes; cook 12-15 minutes

**Each Serving Provides:**
1 Bread
100 Optional Calories

**Per Serving:**
216 Calories
41.2g Carbohydrate
3.6g Fat (0.8g saturated)
2.7g Fiber
6.2g Protein
46mg Cholesterol
404mg Sodium
74mg Calcium
1.3mg Iron

½    cup all-purpose flour
½    cup whole wheat flour
1    teaspoon baking soda
⅛    teaspoon salt
1    tablespoon sugar
1    cup nonfat buttermilk
1    egg, lightly beaten
2    teaspoons vegetable oil
½    cup peeled, finely chopped apple
Vegetable cooking spray
Apple Topping

**1.** Combine first 5 ingredients in a medium bowl; make a well in center of mixture. Combine buttermilk, egg, and oil; add to dry ingredients, stirring just until moistened. Stir in apple. For each pancake, pour ¼ cup batter onto a hot griddle or skillet coated with cooking spray, spreading batter to a 4-inch circle. Cook until tops are bubbly and edges look cooked; turn and cook other side. Top pancakes evenly with Apple Topping. Yield: 10 pancakes (2 pancakes and 3 tablespoons topping per serving).

## Apple Topping

½    cup unsweetened applesauce
½    cup reduced-calorie apple jelly
½    teaspoon apple pie spice

**1.** Combine all ingredients in a small saucepan. Cook over low heat until jelly melts, stirring occasionally. Yield: 1 cup.

# Vanilla Waffles *(photo, page 19)*

**Time:** prep 10 minutes; cook 25 minutes

2¼   cups all-purpose flour
1½   teaspoons baking powder
¼    teaspoon baking soda
¼    teaspoon salt
1     cup nonfat buttermilk
1     (8-ounce) carton vanilla nonfat yogurt
1     egg yolk
1     tablespoon vanilla extract
1     tablespoon vegetable oil
4     egg whites
2     tablespoons sugar
Vegetable cooking spray
1     medium banana, thinly sliced
½    cup reduced-calorie maple syrup

**Each Serving Provides:**

2 Bread
1 Fat

**Per Serving:**

226 Calories
40.0g Carbohydrate
3.2g Fat (0.7g saturated)
1.4g Fiber
8.6g Protein
29mg Cholesterol
200mg Sodium
155mg Calcium
1.9mg Iron

**1.** Combine first 4 ingredients in a large bowl; make a well in center of mixture. Combine buttermilk, yogurt, egg yolk, vanilla, and oil in a medium bowl; stir with a wire whisk. Add to dry ingredients, stirring just until dry ingredients are moistened.

**2.** Beat egg whites at high speed of an electric mixer until soft peaks form. Gradually add 2 tablespoons sugar, beating until stiff peaks form. Gently fold beaten egg white mixture into batter.

**3.** Coat an 8-inch square waffle iron with cooking spray; allow waffle iron to preheat. For each waffle, spoon 1 cup batter onto hot waffle iron, spreading batter to edges. Bake 5 to 6 minutes or until steaming stops. Repeat procedure with remaining batter. Cut each waffle into 4 squares. Top waffles with bananas and maple syrup before serving. Yield: 16 (4-inch) waffles (2 waffles, 5 banana slices, and 1 tablespoon syrup per serving).

## tip

*To keep waffles crisp while remaining waffles cook, place them directly on the rack in a 200° oven.*

# Whole Wheat Carrot Muffins

**Time:** prep 15 minutes; cook 20-25 minutes

| | |
|---|---|
| 1½ | cups whole wheat flour |
| 1½ | cups self-rising flour |
| 2¼ | teaspoons baking powder |
| ¼ | teaspoon salt |
| ¼ | teaspoon ground cinnamon |
| ¼ | teaspoon ground nutmeg |
| ¼ | teaspoon ground allspice |
| ¼ | teaspoon ground ginger |
| 1 | cup shredded carrot |
| ¾ | cup raisins |
| 1 | cup skim milk |
| ½ | cup egg substitute or 2 eggs, lightly beaten |
| ¼ | cup honey |
| 3 | tablespoons margarine, melted |

Vegetable cooking spray

*✿ t i p*

*Look for bags of shredded carrot in the produce section of your supermarket.*

**1.** Combine first 8 ingredients in a large bowl. Add carrot and raisins; stir to combine. Make a well in center of mixture.

**2.** Combine milk, egg substitute, honey, and margarine; add to dry ingredients, stirring just until dry ingredients are moistened.

**3.** Spoon batter into muffin pans coated with cooking spray, filling two-thirds full. Bake at 400° for 20 to 25 minutes. Remove muffins from pans immediately. Yield: 1 dozen (1 muffin per serving).

# Orange-Coconut Muffins

**Time:** prep 12 minutes; cook 20-25 minutes

| | |
|---|---|
| 3 | cups self-rising flour |
| ½ | cup (3 ounces) mixed dried fruit, chopped |
| ¼ | cup firmly packed light brown sugar |
| ¼ | cup shredded coconut |
| 1 | cup orange juice |
| ½ | cup egg substitute or 2 eggs, lightly beaten |
| 3 | tablespoons margarine, melted |
| ¼ | teaspoon lemon extract |

Vegetable cooking spray

**1.** Combine first 4 ingredients in a large bowl; make a well in center of mixture. Combine orange juice, egg substitute, margarine, and lemon extract; add to dry ingredients, stirring just until dry ingredients are moistened.

**2.** Spoon batter into muffin pans coated with cooking spray, filling about two-thirds full. Bake at 400° for 20 to 25 minutes or until golden. Remove muffins from pans immediately. Yield: 1 dozen (1 muffin per serving).

**Each Serving Provides:**

1 Bread
1 Fruit/Vegetable
1 Fat
40 Optional Calories

**Per Serving:**

198 Calories
36.0g Carbohydrate
4.0g Fat (1.3g saturated)
0.6g Fiber
4.4g Protein
0mg Cholesterol
454mg Sodium
119mg Calcium
2.0mg Iron

## ✎ t i p

*It's easier to chop dried fruit if you use kitchen shears sprayed with cooking spray.*

# PB&J Muffins *(photo, page 20)*

**Time:** prep 12 minutes; cook 18-20 minutes

| | |
|---|---|
| 1½ | cups all-purpose flour |
| 2 | teaspoons baking powder |
| ½ | teaspoon salt |
| ¼ | cup firmly packed light brown sugar |
| ⅔ | cup skim milk |
| ½ | cup chunky reduced-fat peanut butter spread |
| ½ | cup egg substitute or 2 eggs |

Vegetable cooking spray

¼  cup plus 2 tablespoons low-sugar fruit spread, any flavor

**1.** Combine first 4 ingredients in a large bowl; make a well in center of mixture.

**2.** Combine milk, peanut butter, and egg substitute in container of an electric blender or food processor. Cover and process until blended.

**3.** Add milk mixture to dry ingredients, stirring just until dry ingredients are moistened.

**4.** Spoon batter into paper-lined muffin pans coated with cooking spray, filling about one-half full; spread batter up sides of each muffin cup. Place 1½ teaspoons fruit spread in center of batter in each muffin cup; cover fruit spread completely with enough batter to fill each muffin cup three-fourths full. Bake at 375° for 18 to 20 minutes or until golden. Serve warm. Yield: 1 dozen (1 muffin per serving).

## tip

*For quicker cleanup, measure sticky ingredients like peanut butter or honey in a measuring cup coated with cooking spray.*

# Whole Wheat Cheese Muffins

**Time:** prep 12 minutes; cook 20-25 minutes

| | |
|---|---|
| 1½ | cups whole wheat flour |
| 1½ | cups self-rising flour |
| 2¼ | teaspoons baking powder |
| ¼ | teaspoon salt |
| ¾ | cup (3 ounces) shredded reduced-fat Cheddar cheese |
| ¼ | cup chopped green onions |
| 1 | teaspoon Italian seasoning |
| 1 | cup skim milk |
| ½ | cup egg substitute or 2 eggs, lightly beaten |
| 3 | tablespoons margarine, melted |

Vegetable cooking spray

**1.** Combine first 7 ingredients in a large bowl; make a well in center of mixture. Combine milk, egg substitute, and margarine; add to dry ingredients, stirring just until dry ingredients are moistened.

**2.** Spoon batter into muffin pans coated with cooking spray, filling two-thirds full. Bake at 400° for 20 to 25 minutes. Yield: 1 dozen (1 muffin per serving).

**Each Serving Provides:**

1 Protein/Milk

1 Bread

1 Fat

**Per Serving:**

167 Calories

24.2g Carbohydrate

4.7g Fat (1.5g saturated)

2g Fiber

7.5g Protein

5mg Cholesterol

360mg Sodium

182mg Calcium

1.8mg Iron

*✎ t i p*

*To save preparation time, buy shredded cheese or grate a large amount at one time and store in a zip-top plastic bag until you're ready to use it.*

# Currant Scones

Time: prep 12 minutes; cook 12-15 minutes

Each Serving Provides:
1 Bread
1 Fat

Per Serving:
98 Calories
13.0g Carbohydrate
4.4g Fat (0.4g saturated)
0.3g Fiber
1.9g Protein
0mg Cholesterol
68mg Sodium
33mg Calcium
0.7mg Iron

✎ *t i p*

*Look for currants on the same aisle with raisins in the supermarket.*

1    cup plus 2 tablespoons all-purpose flour, divided
1    teaspoon baking powder
¼    teaspoon baking soda
Dash of salt
1    tablespoon plus 1½ teaspoons sugar, divided
2    tablespoons stick margarine, chilled
½    cup nonfat buttermilk
2    tablespoons vegetable oil
¼    cup dried currants
Vegetable cooking spray
2    tablespoons egg substitute

**1.** Combine 1 cup flour, baking powder, baking soda, salt, and 1½ teaspoons sugar in a medium bowl. Cut in margarine with a pastry blender until mixture resembles coarse meal.

**2.** Combine buttermilk, oil, and currants; add to flour mixture, stirring with a fork just until blended.

**3.** Sprinkle work surface with remaining 2 tablespoons flour. Turn dough out onto floured surface, and pat to ½-inch thickness. Cut dough into rounds with a 2-inch round biscuit cutter. Place on a baking sheet coated with cooking spray; brush tops with egg substitute. Sprinkle evenly with remaining 1 tablespoon sugar. Bake at 400° for 12 to 15 minutes or until golden. Yield: 1 dozen (1 scone per serving).

# Vegetable-Cheese Scones

**Time:** prep 20 minutes; cook 15-20 minutes

2¼   cups self-rising flour, divided
3     tablespoons stick margarine, chilled
1     cup shredded carrot
1     cup shredded zucchini
¾     cup (3 ounces) shredded reduced-fat Cheddar cheese
¾     cup nonfat buttermilk
Vegetable cooking spray

**1.** Place 2 cups plus 3 tablespoons flour in a large bowl. Cut in margarine with a pastry blender until mixture resembles coarse meal. Stir in carrot, zucchini, and cheese; make a well in center of mixture.

**2.** Add buttermilk to flour mixture; stir until mixture forms a stiff dough. Sprinkle remaining 1 tablespoon flour over work surface. Turn dough out onto floured surface; knead lightly 2 or 3 times.

**3.** Place dough on a baking sheet coated with cooking spray; roll into a circle ¾-inch thick. Using a sharp knife, cut dough into 8 wedges, cutting into but not through dough. Bake at 450° for 15 to 20 minutes or until golden. Yield: 8 scones (1 scone per serving).

**Each Serving Provides:**

1 Protein/Milk
2 Bread
1 Fat

**Per Serving:**

212 Calories
29.4g Carbohydrate
6.8g Fat (2.1g saturated)
0.5g Fiber
7.9g Protein
8mg Cholesterol
605mg Sodium
239mg Calcium
1.8mg Iron

*tip*

Cut preparation time by shredding carrots and zucchini ahead of time. Keep them in a zip-top plastic bag in the refrigerator until ready to use.

# Cheese Sticks

**Time:** prep 20 minutes; cook 15 minutes

*✍ t i p*

*Grate fresh Parmesan cheese and other hard cheeses in the food processor.*

| | |
|---|---|
| 2 | tablespoons all-purpose flour, divided |
| 1 | (10-ounce) package refrigerated pizza dough |
| ¼ | cup plus 2 tablespoons freshly grated Parmesan cheese |
| 2 | teaspoons dried rosemary leaves, crumbled |
| 1 | teaspoon dried thyme leaves |
| ¼ | teaspoon ground red pepper |
| ¼ | teaspoon freshly ground black pepper |

Vegetable cooking spray

**1.** Sprinkle work surface with 1 tablespoon flour. Turn dough out onto floured surface; roll into an 18- x 11-inch rectangle.

**2.** Sprinkle half of dough evenly with Parmesan, rosemary, thyme, red pepper, and black pepper; fold other side of dough over to form an 11-x 9- inch rectangle. Sprinkle evenly with remaining 1 tablespoon flour.

**3.** Press dough with a rolling pin to seal layers, and roll into a 12- x 10-inch rectangle. Cut dough in half lengthwise into two 12- x 5-inch rectangles. Cut a ½-inch-wide strip off short end of one rectangle. Twist strip 6 or 7 times, and place on a baking sheet coated with cooking spray, pressing the ends onto the pan to hold the dough in place. Repeat procedure to make 48 sticks. Bake at 400° for 15 minutes or until golden. Yield: 4 dozen (6 sticks per serving).

Vanilla Waffles (*recipe, page 11*)

19

20 PB&J Muffins *(recipe, page 14)*

Sticky Buns (*recipe, page 25*)

21

Rosemary Focaccia, foreground, *(recipe, page 28)*; Italian Onion Bread *(recipe, page 26)*

# Chile-Cheese Cornbread

**Time:** prep 10 minutes; cook 30 minutes

| | |
|---|---|
| 1 | cup yellow cornmeal |
| 1 | cup all-purpose flour |
| 1 | tablespoon plus 1 teaspoon baking powder |
| ¼ | teaspoon salt |
| ¼ | cup nonfat dry milk powder |
| 1 | tablespoon sugar |
| 1 | cup water |
| ½ | cup egg substitute |
| 2 | tablespoons vegetable oil |
| ¾ | cup (3 ounces) shredded 40% less-fat Cheddar cheese |
| 1 | (4-ounce) can chopped green chiles, drained |

Vegetable cooking spray

**Each Serving Provides:**
1 Bread

**Per Serving:**
107 Calories
15.3g Carbohydrate
3.0g Fat (0.9g saturated)
0.7g Fiber
4.6g Protein
4mg Cholesterol
125mg Sodium
138mg Calcium
1.0mg Iron

**1.** Combine first 6 ingredients in a medium bowl; make a well in center of mixture.

**2.** Combine water, egg substitute, and oil; add to dry ingredients, stirring just until dry ingredients are moistened. Stir in cheese and green chiles.

**3.** Pour batter into an 8-inch square baking dish coated with cooking spray. Bake at 375° for 30 minutes or until cornbread is golden. Yield: 16 servings.

# Cinnamon-Apple Coffee Cake

**Time:** prep 23 minutes; cook 50-55 minutes

2    cups self-rising flour, sifted
½    cup sugar
2    teaspoons ground cinnamon
½    cup egg substitute or 2 eggs
¾    cup skim milk
⅓    cup reduced-calorie margarine, melted
3    small Granny Smith apples, peeled, cored, and diced
⅓    cup raisins
¼    cup chopped walnuts
Vegetable cooking spray

**1.** Combine first 3 ingredients in a medium bowl; set aside.

**2.** Beat egg substitute at medium speed of an electric mixer for 1 minute or until foamy. Add milk and margarine, and beat until mixture is blended.

**3.** Gradually add flour mixture, beating at low speed of mixer just until combined. Stir in apples, raisins, and walnuts.

**4.** Pour batter into an 8-inch round pan coated with cooking spray. Bake at 350° for 50 to 55 minutes, or until a wooden pick inserted in center comes out clean.

**5.** Cool cake in pan on a wire rack 10 minutes. Invert cake onto rack; cool completely. Cut into wedges to serve. Yield: 12 servings (1 wedge per serving).

*tip*

*Out of self-rising flour? Then for each cup, substitute 1 cup all-purpose flour, 1 teaspoon baking powder, and ½ teaspoon salt.*

# Sticky Buns *(photo, page 21)*

**Time:** prep 10 minutes; cook 13 minutes

¼ cup firmly packed dark brown sugar
3 tablespoons reduced-calorie margarine, divided
¼ cup apple juice
Vegetable cooking spray
2 tablespoons finely chopped pecans
2 tablespoons sugar
½ teaspoon ground cinnamon
¼ cup currants
1 (10.8-ounce) can refrigerated reduced-calorie biscuits

**1.** Combine brown sugar, 2 tablespoons margarine, and apple juice in a small saucepan. Bring to a boil; reduce heat, and simmer, uncovered, 8 minutes or until slightly thickened. Pour syrup evenly into 8 muffin pans coated with cooking spray; sprinkle with pecans, and set pans aside.

**2.** Combine sugar, cinnamon, and currants in a small bowl; toss well to coat currants. Set aside.

**3.** Roll biscuits on a lightly floured surface into a 12- x 9-inch rectangle. Spread dough with remaining 1 tablespoon margarine, and sprinkle with currant mixture to within ¼ inch of edge. Roll up dough, starting at short side. Pinch seam to seal (do not seal ends). Cut dough into 8 slices. Place cut sides of slices on top of pecan mixture in muffin pans. Bake at 375° for 12 minutes or until golden. Invert buns onto serving plate; let buns stand, covered with muffin pan, 1 minute. Remove from pan, scraping any remaining pecan mixture from pan onto buns. Serve warm. Yield: 8 buns (1 bun per serving).

**Each Serving Provides:**
1 Bread
1 Fat

**Per Serving:**
215 Calories
32.6g Carbohydrate
8.6g Fat (1.0g saturated)
0.2g Fiber
2.9g Protein
0mg Cholesterol
435mg Sodium
15mg Calcium
0.4mg Iron

*tip*

*When you chop pecans for this recipe, chop extra to freeze and have on hand to use in other recipes.*

# Italian Onion Bread *(photo, page 22)*

**Time:** prep 25 minutes; rise 40 minutes; cook 30 minutes

½    cup warm water (105° to 115°), divided

1    package rapid-rise yeast

¼    teaspoon sugar

1    cup plus 2 tablespoons all-purpose flour, divided

¼    teaspoon salt

¼    teaspoon dried oregano

⅛    teaspoon celery seeds

2    tablespoons sliced green onion tops

Vegetable cooking spray

1    egg white

1    teaspoon water

## tip

*A cold oven or a microwave oven makes a good draft-free place for dough to rise. The fewer drafts, the quicker the dough will rise.*

**1.** Position mixing blade in food processor bowl. Add 2 tablespoons warm water, yeast, and sugar; pulse once or twice. Scrape sides of bowl and let stand 3 minutes, until foamy. Add 1 cup flour, salt, oregano, and celery seeds.

**2.** With processor running, pour remaining ¼ cup plus 2 tablespoons warm water through food chute. Pulse 1 minute or just until dough forms a ball and begins to pull away from sides of bowl. Add green onions, and pulse 6 times to blend onions into dough.

**3.** Place dough in a medium bowl coated with cooking spray, turning to coat top. Cover and let rise in a warm place (85°), free from drafts, 20 minutes or until doubled in bulk.

**4.** Punch dough down. Sprinkle remaining 2 tablespoons flour evenly over work surface. Turn dough out onto floured surface, and knead until smooth and elastic (about 5 minutes). Roll dough into a 14-inch log. Carefully transfer to a baking sheet coated with cooking spray. Coat a sheet of plastic wrap with cooking spray; place lightly over loaf, coated-side down. Let rise 20 minutes.

**5.** Combine egg white and 1 teaspoon water in a small bowl; beat at high speed of an electric mixer just until foamy. Brush evenly with egg white mixture. Bake at 375° for 30 minutes or until loaf sounds hollow when tapped. Transfer to a wire rack immediately, and cool completely. Cut into 8 slices. Yield: 4 servings (2 slices per serving).

## How to Measure Flour for Tender, Low-Fat Breads

If you want to make sure your low-fat breads are tender, not tough, just measure the flour correctly. With less fat to tenderize bread, too much flour will make it tough.

You don't need to sift the flour, but do stir it in the canister to break up clumps.

Lightly spoon the flour into the measuring cup, being sure not to pack it. Don't shake the cup to level it; instead run the edge of a metal spatula across the top of the measuring cup to get a level measure.

The result? Light, tender breads.

# Rosemary Focaccia *(photo, page 22)*

**Time:** prep 15 minutes; rise 1 hour; cook 15-17 minutes

| | |
|---|---|
| 1 | package active dry yeast |
| ½ | cup plus 2 tablespoons warm water (105° to 115°) |
| 1¾ | cups all-purpose flour, divided |
| ¾ | teaspoon salt, divided |
| | Vegetable cooking spray |
| 2 | tablespoons coarsely chopped fresh rosemary |
| 1 | tablespoon olive oil |
| ½ | teaspoon freshly ground black pepper |

**1.** Combine yeast and warm water in a 2-cup liquid measuring cup; let stand 5 minutes. Combine yeast mixture, 1½ cups flour, and ¼ teaspoon salt in a large mixing bowl; beat at medium speed of an electric mixer until well blended.

**2.** Sprinkle remaining ¼ cup flour over work surface. Turn dough out onto floured surface, and knead until smooth and elastic (about 5 minutes). Place in a bowl coated with cooking spray, turning to coat top. Cover and let rise in a warm place (85°), free from drafts, 1 hour or until doubled in bulk.

**3.** Punch dough down. Pat dough into an 8-inch circle (about ¼-inch-thick) on a baking sheet coated with cooking spray. Poke holes in dough at 1-inch intervals with handle of a wooden spoon. Sprinkle dough with remaining ½ teaspoon salt and rosemary. Drizzle evenly with olive oil, and sprinkle evenly with pepper. Bake at 450° for 15 to 17 minutes or until golden. Cut focaccia into 8 wedges. Yield: 8 servings (1 wedge per serving).

## tip

*Use a small food chopper or a food processor to chop fresh rosemary quickly. Pulse lightly to keep from overprocessing.*

*fish*

*&*

*shellfish*

# Baked Fish with Chile Sauce

**Time:** prep 15 minutes; cook 25 minutes

| | |
|---|---|
| 4 | (4-ounce) flounder or other white fish fillets |
| 1 | small onion, sliced |
| ½ | cup water |
| ¼ | cup vermouth |
| 1 | tablespoon fresh lime juice |
| 2 | teaspoons margarine |
| ¼ | cup finely chopped mild green chiles |
| 2 | teaspoons all-purpose flour |
| ½ | teaspoon vegetable bouillon granules |
| 1 | tablespoon chopped fresh cilantro |

*✎ t i p*

*It's okay to substitute canned green chiles for fresh ones. Just drain and measure.*

**1.** Arrange fish in an 8-inch square pan; top with onion.

**2.** Combine water, vermouth, and lime juice; pour over fish. Cover and bake at 350° for 20 minutes or until fish flakes easily when tested with a fork.

**3.** Place fish on a serving platter; keep warm. Strain pan juices, and set aside.

**4.** Heat margarine in a medium skillet over medium-high heat until melted. Add chiles and cook, stirring constantly, 30 seconds. Stir in flour; remove skillet from heat. Gradually add reserved pan juices, stirring constantly.

**5.** Return skillet to medium-high heat; add bouillon granules. Cook, stirring constantly, 3 minutes or until thickened. Stir in cilantro.

**6.** Pour chile mixture over fish. Yield: 4 servings.

# Spicy Lime Fish

**Time:** prep 8 minutes; marinate 1 hour; cook 10 minutes

4     (4-ounce) flounder or other white fish fillets
1     teaspoon grated lime rind
1     tablespoon fresh lime juice
¼    teaspoon crushed red pepper flakes
½    teaspoon dried dillweed
Vegetable cooking spray

**1.** Place fish in a shallow dish. Combine lime rind and next 3 ingredients in a small bowl; brush over fish. Cover and marinate in refrigerator at least 1 hour.

**2.** Arrange fish in a grilling basket coated with cooking spray. Place on grill rack over medium-hot coals (350° to 400°); grill, uncovered, 5 minutes on each side or until fish flakes easily when tested with a fork. Yield: 4 servings.

**Each Serving Provides:**

1 Protein/Milk
40 Optional Calories

**Per Serving:**

103 Calories
0.6g Carbohydrate
1.5g Fat (0.3g saturated)
0.1g Fiber
20.6g Protein
58mg Cholesterol
90mg Sodium
19mg Calcium
0.4mg Iron

*tip*

*You'll find it's easier to grate the rind while the lime is whole. Extract the juice after grating the rind.*

# Garlic Flounder

**Time:** prep 10 minutes; marinate 30 minutes; cook 8-10 minutes

| | |
|---|---|
| 6 | (4-ounce) flounder fillets |
| ¼ | cup low-sodium soy sauce |
| 2 | tablespoons minced garlic |
| 1½ | tablespoons lemon juice |
| 2 | teaspoons sugar |
| 1 | tablespoon mixed peppercorns, crushed |

Vegetable cooking spray

**1.** Place fish in a shallow baking dish. Combine soy sauce and next 3 ingredients; pour over fish. Cover and marinate in refrigerator 30 minutes.

**2.** Remove fish from marinade; discard marinade. Sprinkle fish evenly with peppercorns, pressing firmly so pepper adheres to fish.

**3.** Place fish on rack of a broiler pan coated with cooking spray. Broil 5½ inches from heat (with electric oven door partially opened) 8 to 10 minutes or until fish flakes easily when tested with a fork. Yield: 6 servings.

## tip

*If you don't have mixed pepper-corns, just use cracked black peppercorns or coarsely ground black pepper.*

# Stir-Fried Fish with Orange Sauce

**Time:** prep 10 minutes; cook 10 minutes

| | |
|---|---|
| 1 | pound orange roughy or other white fish fillets |
| 3 | tablespoons all-purpose flour |
| | Vegetable cooking spray |
| 2 | teaspoons vegetable oil |
| 1 | cup thinly sliced celery |
| 1 | cup orange juice |
| 3 | tablespoons water |
| 1 | tablespoon plus 1 teaspoon cornstarch |
| 1 | tablespoon low-sodium soy sauce |
| 2 | teaspoons peeled, grated gingerroot |
| 1 | teaspoon grated fresh orange rind |
| 8 | medium-size green onions, chopped |

**1.** Cut fish into 1-inch strips. Place flour in a large heavy-duty, zip-top plastic bag; add fish. Seal bag, and shake gently to coat fish.

**2.** Coat a wok or large nonstick skillet with cooking spray; drizzle oil around top of wok, coating sides. Heat at medium-high (375°) until hot. Add fish, and stir-fry 2 minutes or until lightly browned. Remove fish from wok; set aside.

**3.** Add celery to wok; stir-fry 2 minutes or until crisp-tender. Combine orange juice and remaining 6 ingredients. Add to wok; bring to a boil, and cook, stirring constantly, 3 minutes or until thickened. Return fish to wok; stir to coat. Transfer mixture to a serving platter. Yield: 4 servings.

**Each Serving Provides:**

2 Protein/Milk

1 Fruit/Vegetable

1 Fat

**Per Serving:**

171 Calories

16.0g Carbohydrate

3.4g Fat (0.5g saturated)

1.1g Fiber

18.2g Protein

23mg Cholesterol

198mg Sodium

30mg Calcium

0.9mg Iron

*tip*

*Make quick work of slicing celery by cutting 3 or 4 stalks at one time.*

# Sweet-and-Sour Fish Rolls

**Time:** prep 10 minutes; cook 15-20 minutes

**Each Serving Provides:**
2 Protein/Milk
1 Bread

**Per Serving:**
171 Calories
20.5g Carbohydrate
1.5g Fat (0.1g saturated)
1.4g Fiber
18.4g Protein
23mg Cholesterol
210mg Sodium
13mg Calcium
0.7mg Iron

Vegetable cooking spray
4    (4-ounce) orange roughy or other white fish fillets
1    cup cooked brown rice (cooked without salt or fat)
¼    cup canned crushed pineapple in juice, drained
¼    cup chopped green onions
¼    cup chopped sweet red pepper
3    tablespoons ketchup
2    teaspoons honey
2    teaspoons fresh lemon juice
Fresh lemon wedges

**1.** Cut four 10-inch square pieces of aluminum foil; coat one side of each with cooking spray. Arrange one fish fillet in the center of each piece of foil.

**2.** Combine rice and next 6 ingredients. Spread one-fourth of mixture over each fillet. Fold in sides of each fillet; roll up, and secure with wooden picks. Wrap each fish roll in aluminum foil, sealing ends of foil securely.

**3.** Place foil packets in an 8-inch square pan, and bake at 350° for 15 to 20 minutes or until fish flakes easily when tested with a fork.

**4.** Remove fish rolls from foil; arrange on a serving platter. Serve with lemon wedges. Yield: 4 servings.

## ✦ *tip*

*Use leftover brown rice for this recipe, or cook the rice a day ahead of time. One-third cup of uncooked rice will yield 1 to 1¼ cups of cooked rice.*

# Fettuccine with Salmon Sauce

**Time:** prep 15 minutes; cook 10 minutes

9    ounces fettuccine, uncooked
Vegetable cooking spray
2    teaspoons vegetable oil
1    small onion, sliced
4    cloves garlic, minced
2    (16-ounce) cans no-salt-added tomatoes, drained and chopped
½    cup tomato puree
Dash of dried oregano
Dash of freshly ground pepper
2    drops hot sauce
1    (16-ounce) can salmon, drained and flaked
½    cup (2 ounces) shredded reduced-fat Cheddar cheese

**1.** Cook fettuccine according to package directions, omitting salt and fat. Drain well, and keep warm.

**2.** Coat a large skillet with cooking spray; add oil, and place skillet over medium-high heat until hot. Add onion and garlic, and sauté 3 minutes or until tender. Add tomato and next 4 ingredients; cook 5 minutes, stirring occasionally. Stir in salmon; cook until salmon is thoroughly heated.

**3.** Arrange fettuccine on a serving platter. Top with salmon mixture; sprinkle with cheese. Yield: 6 servings.

**Each Serving Provides:**
2 Protein/Milk
2 Bread
1 Fruit/Vegetable
40 Optional Calories

**Per Serving:**
338 Calories
40.7g Carbohydrate
9.5g Fat (2.3g saturated)
1.2g Fiber
23.2g Protein
33mg Cholesterol
249mg Sodium
281mg Calcium
1.6mg Iron

*tip*

*Use kitchen shears to chop tomatoes right in the can to save cleanup and time.*

# Tuna and Corn Pie

**Time:** prep 15 minutes; chill 20 minutes; cook 35-45 minutes

| | |
|---|---|
| 1 | cup whole wheat flour |
| 3 | tablespoons stick margarine, chilled |
| 2 | tablespoons ice water |
| 2 | tablespoons all-purpose flour |
| | Vegetable cooking spray |
| 1 | teaspoon margarine |
| 1 | medium-size green or sweet red pepper, seeded and chopped |
| ½ | cup thinly sliced leek |
| ½ | cup canned whole kernel corn, drained |
| 2 | (6.5-ounce) cans water-packed tuna, drained and flaked |
| ½ | cup skim milk |
| ½ | cup egg substitute |
| 1 | tablespoon chopped fresh parsley |
| | Dash of freshly ground pepper |

*✎ t i p*

*After snipping a tablespoon of parsley from a bunch for this recipe, chop the remainder. Then store the extra in an airtight bag in the freezer for up to 2 months.*

**1.** Pour whole wheat flour into a small bowl; cut in 3 tablespoons margarine with a pastry blender until mixture resembles coarse meal. Sprinkle ice water, 1 teaspoon at a time, over flour mixture, tossing with a fork until mixture forms a soft dough. Cover and refrigerate for 15 to 20 minutes.

**2.** Sprinkle rolling pin and work surface with 2 tablespoons all-purpose flour. Turn dough out onto work surface. Roll dough out to ⅛-inch thickness. Place pastry in a 9-inch pieplate coated with cooking spray. Trim off excess pastry along edges. Fold edges of pastry under, and flute.

**3.** Prick bottom and sides of pastry generously with a fork. Bake at 400° for 10 to 15 minutes or until lightly browned.

**4.** Heat 1 teaspoon margarine in a medium skillet over medium-high heat until melted. Add green pepper and leek; sauté 5 minutes or until tender. Remove skillet from heat; stir in corn and remaining 5 ingredients.

**5.** Spoon tuna mixture into baked pastry shell, and bake at 350° for 25 to 30 minutes. Yield: 6 servings.

## Fish in a Flash

One of the fastest ways to cook fish is in the microwave. Because of its high moisture content, fish cooks quickly and keeps its fresh flavor. Use these tips for tender, flaky fish.

• Cook 4 (4-ounce) fish fillets on HIGH for 5 to 8 minutes.

• Place the thickest part of fish fillets on the outside edges of the dish.

• Tuck under any especially thin edges of fillets to avoid overcooking.

• Always cook fish for the minimum time suggested; then continue cooking 15 seconds at a time to complete cooking, if necessary. It is easy to overcook fish.

• You'll know fish is cooked when it is opaque and flakes easily with a fork.

# Honeyed Shrimp Stir-Fry *(photo, facing page)*

**Time:** prep 20 minutes; cook 7 minutes

1½   pounds unpeeled medium-size fresh shrimp
Vegetable cooking spray
2    teaspoons sesame oil
2    teaspoons peeled, grated gingerroot
2    cloves garlic, minced
1    (8-ounce) package Sugar Snap peas
¼    cup honey
1    tablespoon low-sodium soy sauce
1    tablespoon sesame seeds, toasted
6    cups hot cooked rice (cooked without salt or fat)

**1.** Peel and devein shrimp, leaving tails intact, if desired.

**2.** Coat a wok or large nonstick skillet with cooking spray; drizzle oil around top of wok, coating sides. Heat at medium-high (375°) until hot. Add gingerroot and garlic; stir-fry 30 seconds. Add shrimp, and stir-fry 3 minutes. Add Sugar Snap peas; stir-fry 2 minutes or until peas are crisp-tender and shrimp turn pink.

**3.** Combine honey and soy sauce, stirring well. Gradually add honey mixture to wok, stirring constantly; cook, stirring constantly, 2 minutes or until thoroughly heated. Stir in sesame seeds. Serve over rice. Yield: 6 servings.

## ☙ *t i p*

*To toast sesame seeds, place them in a hot skillet (without oil), and stir 1 to 2 minutes or until toasted.*

Honeyed Shrimp Stir-Fry *(recipe, facing page)*

Asparagus Quiche *(recipe, page 49)*

Mushroom Pizza *(recipe, page 56)*

Snow Pea and Pepper Salad *(recipe, page 64)* and Gingered Fruit Cup *(recipe, page 166)*

# Lemon Shrimp Kabobs

**Time:** prep 10 minutes; marinate 1 hour; cook 8 minutes

1⅓  pounds unpeeled medium-size fresh shrimp
½  cup cold tea
3  tablespoons fresh lemon juice
2  teaspoons olive oil
2  cloves garlic, minced
16  cherry tomatoes
½  medium-size green pepper, seeded and cut into 8 equal pieces
Vegetable cooking spray
2  cups hot cooked rice (cooked without salt or fat)

**1.** Peel and devein shrimp, leaving tails intact, if desired.

**2.** Combine tea and next 3 ingredients in a large heavy-duty, zip-top plastic bag; add shrimp. Seal and turn to coat shrimp; marinate in refrigerator 1 to 2 hours, turning bag occasionally.

**3.** Drain marinade into a small saucepan; bring to a boil. Remove from heat, and set aside. Thread shrimp, cherry tomatoes, and green pepper pieces evenly onto 8 (8-inch) skewers. Place kabobs on rack of a broiler pan coated with cooking spray. Brush kabobs with boiled marinade.

**4.** Broil kabobs 5½ inches from heat (with electric oven door partially opened) 4 minutes. Turn and baste with remaining marinade; broil 4 additional minutes or until shrimp turn pink and vegetables are tender.

**5.** Spoon ½ cup rice onto each of 4 plates; top each with 2 shrimp kabobs. Yield: 4 servings.

**Each Serving Provides:**
2 Protein/Milk
1 Bread
1 Fat

**Per Serving:**
253 Calories
26.1g Carbohydrate
4.7g Fat (0.7g saturated)
1.4g Fiber
25.4g Protein
172mg Cholesterol
175mg Sodium
75mg Calcium
4.0mg Iron

*tip*

*You'll get more juice from a lemon if you let it come to room temperature first and then roll it against the counter with the palm of your hand.*

# Shrimp and Pepper Stir-Fry

**Time:** prep 20 minutes; cook 9 minutes

| | |
|---|---|
| 1½ | pounds unpeeled medium-size fresh shrimp |
| | Vegetable cooking spray |
| 2 | teaspoons olive oil |
| 2 | cups sweet red pepper strips |
| 1 | cup green pepper strips |
| 1 | tablespoon chopped green onions |
| 2 | cloves garlic, minced |
| 1 | tablespoon fresh lemon juice |
| 1 | tablespoon white wine vinegar |
| ¼ | cup chopped fresh parsley |
| ½ | teaspoon dried basil |

**1.** Peel and devein shrimp; set aside.

**2.** Coat a wok or large nonstick skillet with cooking spray; drizzle oil around top of wok, coating sides. Heat at medium-high (375°) until hot. Add peppers, green onions, and garlic; stir-fry 4 minutes or until vegetables are tender.

**3.** Add shrimp, lemon juice, vinegar, parsley, and basil; stir-fry 5 minutes or until shrimp turn pink. Yield: 6 servings.

## 🌿 *tip*

*Most stores will peel and devein shrimp for you. It may cost a little extra, but you'll save a lot of time.*

# Creamy Fettuccine with Shrimp

**Time:** prep 12 minutes; cook 15 minutes

½   pound unpeeled large fresh shrimp (about 12 shrimp)
3   ounces spinach fettuccine, uncooked
3   ounces plain fettuccine, uncooked
1   cup nonfat cottage cheese
½   cup evaporated skimmed milk
¾   cup freshly grated Parmesan cheese
½   cup water
2   teaspoons crab boil seasoning
2   teaspoons margarine
2   cups sliced mushrooms
1   cup chopped green onions
1   cup diced tomato

**Each Serving Provides:**

3 Protein/Milk

2 Bread

1 Fruit/Vegetable

1 Fat

**Per Serving:**

398 Calories

41.8g Carbohydrate

10.5g Fat (4.8g saturated)

3.2g Fiber

34.5g Protein

85mg Cholesterol

55mg Sodium

498mg Calcium

4.5mg Iron

**1.** Peel and devein shrimp; set aside.

**2.** Cook fettuccine according to package directions, omitting salt and fat. Drain fettuccine, and place in a serving bowl; keep warm.

**3.** Position knife blade in food processor bowl; add cottage cheese, milk, and cheese. Process until smooth; set mixture aside.

**4.** Combine water and crab boil seasoning in a large nonstick skillet; bring to a boil. Add shrimp to boiling water, and cook 1 minute or until shrimp turn pink. Drain and set aside.

**5.** Heat margarine in skillet over medium-high heat until melted. Add mushrooms and green onions, and cook, stirring constantly, 5 minutes or until tender. Reduce heat to medium; add tomato, shrimp, and cottage cheese mixture. Cook, stirring gently, for 2 minutes or until thoroughly heated. Add shrimp mixture to fettuccine; toss well. Yield: 4 servings.

*tip*

*Buy sliced mushrooms instead of whole ones to save preparation time.*

# Seafood Spaghetti in Wine Sauce

**Time:** prep 10 minutes; cook 15 minutes

**Each Serving Provides:**
3 Protein/Milk
2 Bread
1 Fat

**Per Serving:**
372 Calories
40.1g Carbohydrate
7.2g Fat (1.2g saturated)
0.1g Fiber
34.8g Protein
165mg Cholesterol
366mg Sodium
164mg Calcium
5.2mg Iron

| | |
|---|---|
| 6 | ounces spaghetti, uncooked |
| 1 | pound unpeeled medium-size fresh shrimp |
| 1 | tablespoon margarine |
| 2 | cloves garlic, minced |
| ½ | cup dry white wine |
| ¼ | cup water |
| 1 | tablespoon plus 1 teaspoon cornstarch |
| ¾ | cup plain nonfat yogurt |
| 1 | teaspoon fresh lemon juice |

Dash of salt
Dash of pepper

| | |
|---|---|
| ½ | (12-ounce) container fresh standard oysters, drained |
| 5 | ounces sea scallops, halved |
| 1 | tablespoon chopped fresh parsley |

## ✿ t i p

*For the fastest cooking pasta, use fresh pasta, which is found in the refrigerated section of supermarkets. It cooks in just 2 to 3 minutes.*

**1.** Cook spaghetti according to package directions, omitting salt and fat. Drain and transfer to a serving platter; keep warm.

**2.** Peel and devein shrimp; set aside.

**3.** Heat margarine in a large nonstick skillet over medium-high heat until melted. Add garlic, and cook, stirring constantly, 1 minute. Add wine; bring to a boil, and cook 3 minutes.

**4.** Combine ¼ cup water and cornstarch in a small bowl, stirring until cornstarch is dissolved. Stir in yogurt, mixing well. Add yogurt mixture to skillet, and cook, stirring constantly, 3 minutes or until thickened and bubbly. Stir in lemon juice, salt, and pepper. Stir oysters, shrimp, and scallops into sauce; cook 2 minutes or until oysters curl, shrimp turn pink, and scallops are opaque. Top spaghetti with seafood mixture, and sprinkle with parsley. Yield: 4 servings.

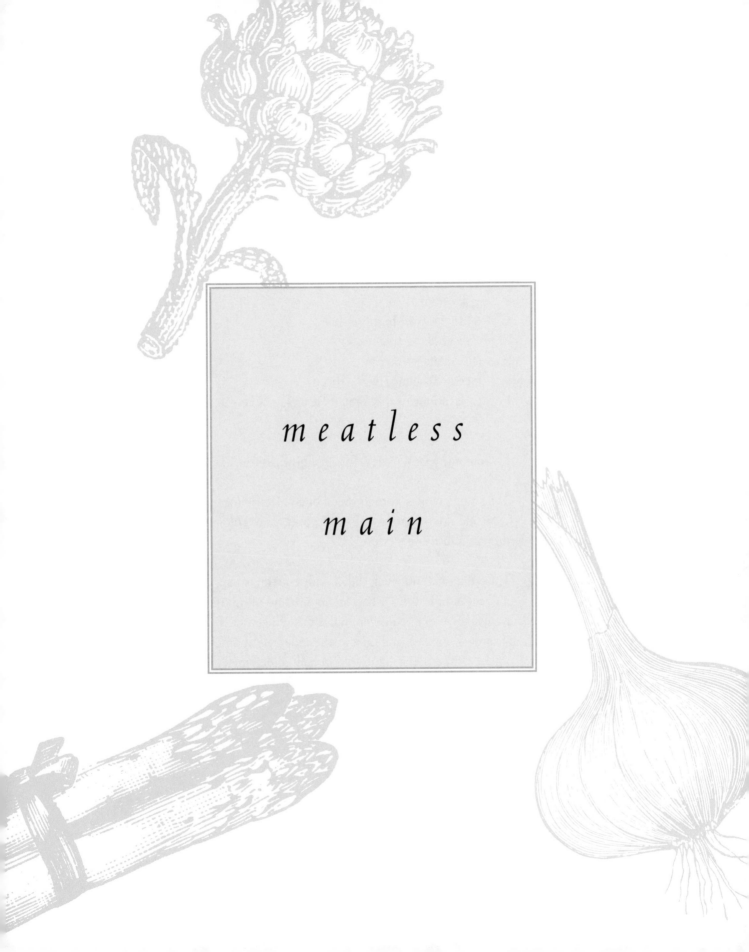

*meatless*

*main*

# Garden-Fresh Omelets

**Time:** prep 8 minutes; cook 10 minutes

½     cup egg substitute
2     tablespoons skim milk
1½    teaspoons minced fresh dillweed
⅛     teaspoon pepper
4     egg whites
1     tablespoon all-purpose flour
Vegetable cooking spray
½     cup alfalfa sprouts
1     medium tomato, thinly sliced
1½    tablespoons freshly grated Parmesan cheese

**1.** Combine first 4 ingredients in a bowl; stir well, and set aside.

**2.** Beat egg whites at high speed of an electric mixer until soft peaks form; add flour, beating until stiff peaks form. Fold egg white mixture into egg substitute mixture.

**3.** Coat a small nonstick skillet with cooking spray; place over medium heat until hot. Pour half of egg mixture into skillet, spreading evenly. Cover and cook 5 minutes or until center is set. Arrange half of sprouts, tomato, and cheese over one half of omelet. Loosen omelet with a spatula, and fold in half. Slide omelet onto a warm serving plate. Repeat procedure with remaining half of egg mixture, sprouts, tomato, and cheese. Yield: 2 servings.

## ✐ *tip*

*To get thin, clean-cut slices of tomato, use a sharp knife with a serrated blade.*

# Asparagus Quiche *(photo, page 40)*

**Time:** prep 10 minutes; cook 45 minutes

| | |
|---|---|
| 3 | tablespoons margarine, melted |
| 24 | unsalted crackers, crushed |
| 1½ | cups evaporated skimmed milk |
| 1 | cup egg substitute |
| 1 | teaspoon dry mustard |
| 1 | teaspoon Worcestershire sauce |
| ⅛ | teaspoon ground nutmeg |

Dash of freshly ground pepper

| | |
|---|---|
| 1 | pound fresh asparagus, trimmed and cut into 1½-inch pieces (about 2½ cups) |

**1.** Combine margarine and crackers; press mixture in bottom and up sides of a 10-inch pieplate. Bake at 350° for 5 minutes; set aside.

**2.** Combine milk and next 5 ingredients; stir in asparagus. Pour mixture into prepared crust; bake at 350° for 30 to 35 minutes or until set. Let stand 10 minutes before serving. Yield: 6 servings.

**Each Serving Provides:**

1 Protein/Milk

1 Bread

1 Fat

**Per Serving:**

184 Calories

18.7g Carbohydrate

7.6g Fat (1.2g saturated)

1.2g Fiber

11.1g Protein

3mg Cholesterol

291mg Sodium

214mg Calcium

1.7mg Iron

*tip*

*Seal crackers in a heavy-duty, zip-top plastic bag and use a rolling pin or meat mallet to crush them.*

# Crustless Chile Quiche

Time: prep 10 minutes; cook 40 minutes

**Each Serving Provides:**

1 Protein/Milk

60 Optional Calories

**Per Serving:**

98 Calories

5.7g Carbohydrate

2.8g Fat (1.6g saturated)

0.2g Fiber

12.1g Protein

8mg Cholesterol

355mg Sodium

103mg Calcium

1.0mg Iron

| | |
|---|---|
| 1 | cup egg substitute |
| 3 | tablespoons all-purpose flour |
| 2 | tablespoons reduced-calorie margarine, melted |
| 1 | tablespoon Dijon mustard |
| 1/8 | teaspoon hot sauce |
| 1 | cup nonfat cottage cheese |
| 1/4 | cup plus 2 tablespoons (1 1/2 ounces) shredded reduced-fat Monterey Jack cheese |
| 1/4 | cup canned chopped green chiles |
| 1/4 | cup chopped roasted red pepper |

Vegetable cooking spray

| | |
|---|---|
| 1 | tablespoon freshly grated Parmesan cheese |

**1.** Combine first 5 ingredients in a bowl, stirring well with a wire whisk. Stir in cottage cheese, Monterey Jack cheese, green chiles, and roasted red pepper. Pour mixture into a 9-inch pieplate coated with cooking spray; sprinkle with Parmesan cheese.

**2.** Bake at 350° for 30 to 32 minutes or until set. Let stand 10 minutes before serving. Yield: 6 servings.

## *tip*

*If you don't have time to roast your own peppers, buy roasted peppers in jars instead. Look for them on the condiments aisle in your supermarket.*

# Spinach Pie with Rice Crust

**Time:** prep 10 minutes; cook 40 minutes

| | |
|---|---|
| 2 | cups cooked brown rice (cooked without salt or fat) |
| ¾ | cup egg substitute, divided |
| ½ | cup finely chopped onion |
| 1 | tablespoon margarine, melted |
| | Vegetable cooking spray |
| ⅓ | cup evaporated skimmed milk |
| ⅛ | teaspoon salt |
| ⅛ | teaspoon white pepper |
| 2 | cups drained cooked spinach |
| ⅔ | cup (2.6 ounces) shredded Swiss cheese |
| 1 | medium tomato, sliced |

**1.** Combine rice, ¼ cup egg substitute, onion, and margarine; press mixture into bottom and up the sides of a 9-inch pieplate coated with cooking spray. Set aside.

**2.** Combine remaining ½ cup egg substitute, milk, salt, and pepper; stir in spinach and cheese.

**3.** Pour spinach mixture into prepared rice crust; arrange tomato slices around edge of pie. Bake at 350° for 30 minutes or until set. Let stand 10 minutes before serving. Yield: 4 servings.

**Each Serving Provides:**

2 Protein/Milk

1 Bread

1 Fruit/Vegetable

1 Fat

**Per Serving:**

279 Calories

32.8g Carbohydrate

9.3g Fat (4.1g saturated)

4.9g Fiber

17.1g Protein

18mg Cholesterol

315mg Sodium

392mg Calcium

4.7mg Iron

*tip*

*Select bags of washed and trimmed spinach to save time. One pound of fresh spinach yields about 2 cups of cooked spinach.*

# Vegetarian Chili

**Time:** prep 10 minutes; cook 33 minutes

**Each Serving Provides:**
1 Protein/Milk
1 Bread
1 Fruit/Vegetable

**Per Serving:**
236 Calories
48.2g Carbohydrate
2.5g Fat (0.3g saturated)
7.8g Fiber
11.2g Protein
0mg Cholesterol
122mg Sodium
80mg Calcium
3.2mg Iron

Vegetable cooking spray
1 teaspoon vegetable oil
2¼ cups chopped onion
1 tablespoon chili powder
¼ teaspoon ground cumin
⅛ teaspoon ground cinnamon
1¼ cups chopped plum tomatoes
1 cup no-salt-added tomato juice
½ cup diced green pepper
2 jalapeño peppers, seeded and minced
1 (15-ounce) can kidney or red beans, drained
2 cups fresh or frozen corn kernels, thawed
¼ cup plain nonfat yogurt
1 tablespoon chopped fresh cilantro

*✍ t i p*

*The pickled jalapeño peppers that come in a jar can be substituted for fresh ones, and they won't taste "pickled." Store the opened jar in the refrigerator.*

**1.** Coat a large nonstick skillet with cooking spray, and add oil; place over medium-high heat until hot. Add onion, and cook 10 minutes or until tender, stirring often.

**2.** Add chili powder, cumin, and cinnamon; cook 3 minutes, stirring often. Stir in tomatoes and next 4 ingredients. Reduce heat to low; cover and simmer 15 minutes, stirring occasionally.

**3.** Stir in corn; simmer 5 minutes or until corn is thoroughly heated. Ladle chili into individual bowls. Top each serving with 1 tablespoon yogurt; sprinkle evenly with cilantro. Yield: 4 servings.

# Red-Hot Beans and Rice

**Time:** prep 15 minutes; cook 15 minutes

Vegetable cooking spray
| | |
|---|---|
| 2 | teaspoons vegetable oil |
| 1 | cup chopped onion |
| 1 | cup chopped green pepper |
| 2 | cloves garlic, crushed |
| 1 | cup chopped tomato |
| 1 | cup frozen corn kernels, thawed |
| 1 | cup sliced mushrooms |
| 1 | cup no-salt-added tomato sauce |
| ½ | cup water |
| ¼ | teaspoon salt |
| ¼ | teaspoon ground red pepper |
| ¼ | teaspoon ground cumin |
| 1 | (15-ounce) can red kidney beans, drained |
| 2 | cups hot cooked brown rice (cooked without salt or fat) |
| ¼ | cup nonfat sour cream |

**Each Serving Provides:**

1 Protein/Milk

1 Bread

1 Fruit/Vegetable

1 Fat

**Per Serving:**

313 Calories

59.6g Carbohydrate

4.2g Fat (0.7g saturated)

8.0g Fiber

12.3g Protein

0mg Cholesterol

259mg Sodium

45mg Calcium

3.4mg Iron

**1.** Coat a large nonstick skillet with cooking spray, and add oil; place over medium heat until hot. Add onion, green pepper, and garlic; cook 5 minutes or until tender, stirring occasionally.

**2.** Stir in chopped tomato and next 8 ingredients; simmer, uncovered, 10 minutes.

**3.** To serve, place ½ cup cooked rice in each of 4 individual serving bowls; spoon bean mixture evenly over rice, and top each serving with 1 tablespoon sour cream. Yield: 4 servings.

*✎ t i p*

*Keep commercial packages of frozen chopped onion and chopped green pepper in the freezer to measure out quickly.*

# Chunky Minestrone

**Time:** prep 10 minutes; cook 28 minutes

Vegetable cooking spray

2 teaspoons olive oil

1½ cups chopped onion

1 medium carrot, halved lengthwise and sliced

1 clove garlic, minced

½ cup long-grain rice, uncooked

2½ cups water

1¼ cups no-salt-added canned vegetable broth, undiluted

2 (14½-ounce) cans no-salt-added whole tomatoes, undrained and chopped

1 teaspoon dried Italian seasoning

1 medium zucchini, halved lengthwise and sliced

1 (15-ounce) can cannellini beans, drained

1 (10-ounce) package frozen chopped spinach, thawed and drained

¼ teaspoon pepper

⅔ cup freshly grated Parmesan cheese

**1.** Coat a Dutch oven with cooking spray, and add oil; place over medium-high heat until hot. Add onion, carrot, and garlic; cook 3 minutes, stirring occasionally.

**2.** Add rice and next 4 ingredients to Dutch oven; bring to a boil. Cover, reduce heat, and simmer 20 minutes. Add zucchini and next 3 ingredients; cook 5 additional minutes. Ladle into individual soup bowls, and sprinkle evenly with cheese. Yield: 7 servings.

## ✿ t i p

*Thaw frozen spinach in the microwave at LOW (30% power) for 5 minutes. Break it apart with a fork and continue defrosting, 1 minute at a time, until it's thawed.*

# Curried Vegetable-Rice Pilaf

**Time:** prep 10 minutes; cook 20 minutes

Vegetable cooking spray
2　teaspoons vegetable oil
2　cups cauliflower flowerets
2　cups cubed unpeeled eggplant
1　cup green pepper strips
1　cup chopped onion
2　cloves garlic, crushed
½　cup water
2　cups no-salt-added stewed tomatoes
1½　teaspoons curry powder
¼　teaspoon salt
1　(15½-ounce) can chickpeas, drained
2　tablespoons golden raisins
Dash of ground cinnamon
2　cups hot cooked brown rice (cooked without salt or fat)

**Each Serving Provides:**
1 Protein/Milk
1 Bread
2 Fruit/Vegetable
1 Fat

**Per Serving:**
344 Calories
64.6g Carbohydrate
5.6g Fat (1.0g saturated)
9.5g Fiber
12.6g Protein
0mg Cholesterol
266mg Sodium
123mg Calcium
4.4mg Iron

**1.** Coat a large nonstick skillet with cooking spray, and add oil; place over medium heat until hot. Add cauliflower and next 4 ingredients to skillet, and cook 5 minutes or until lightly browned, stirring occasionally. Add ½ cup water; cover, and simmer 5 additional minutes or until vegetables are tender.

**2.** Stir in tomatoes, curry powder, salt, and chickpeas; simmer, uncovered, 10 minutes.

**3.** Stir raisins and cinnamon into rice in a large bowl; add vegetable mixture, stirring well to combine. Yield: 4 servings.

*tip*

*To save time, purchase packages of cauliflower flowerets. Find them in the produce section of your supermarket.*

# Mushroom Pizza *(photo, page 41)*

**Time:** prep 10 minutes; cook 5 minutes

**Each Serving Provides:**
1 Protein/Milk
1 Bread
2 Fruit/Vegetable

**Per Serving:**
304 Calories
47.3g Carbohydrate
6.8g Fat (3.1g saturated)
9.7g Fiber
13.6g Protein
16mg Cholesterol
160mg Sodium
305mg Calcium
6.1mg Iron

| | |
|---|---|
| 2 | tablespoons tomato paste |
| 1 | teaspoon Italian seasoning |
| 1 | clove garlic, minced |
| 1 | (7-inch) pita bread round |
| ½ | cup sliced mushrooms |
| ¼ | cup thinly sliced onion |
| ⅓ | cup sliced sweet red pepper |
| ⅓ | cup sliced green pepper |
| ¼ | cup (1 ounce) shredded part-skim mozzarella cheese |

**1.** Combine first 3 ingredients; spread evenly over pita bread.

**2.** Arrange mushrooms, onion, and peppers over tomato paste mixture; sprinkle with cheese.

**3.** Place pizza on an ungreased baking sheet; broil 5½ inches from heat (with electric oven door partially opened) 5 minutes or until golden. Yield: 1 serving.

✎ *t i p*

*Pick up already-cut vegetables from the salad bar in your supermarket to make this pizza in even less time.*

# Creamy Primavera-Stuffed Potatoes

**Time:** prep 12 minutes; cook 26 minutes

| | |
|---|---|
| 4 | (5-ounce) baking potatoes, scrubbed |
| 2 | cups coarsely chopped zucchini |
| 1 | cup thinly sliced carrot |
| 1 | cup chopped green onions |
| ¼ | cup water |
| 1 | cup chopped roasted red peppers |
| ¼ | cup plus 2 tablespoons (1½ ounces) shredded nonfat Cheddar cheese |
| ¼ | cup nonfat sour cream |
| 1 | tablespoon Dijon mustard |
| 1 | tablespoon fresh lemon juice |
| 1 | teaspoon salt-free lemon-herb seasoning |

**1.** Pierce potatoes with a fork. Arrange in a circle on paper towels in microwave oven. Microwave at HIGH for 12 to 14 minutes, turning and rearranging potatoes after 6 minutes. Let stand 5 minutes.

**2.** Combine zucchini, carrot, green onions, and water in a microwave-safe 2-quart casserole. Cover and microwave at HIGH for 4 to 5 minutes, stirring once; let stand, covered, 5 minutes. Drain.

**3.** Combine roasted peppers and remaining ingredients; add to zucchini mixture, stirring well to combine. Cut a deep cross in top of each potato, and squeeze lightly to open. Spoon vegetable topping evenly over potatoes; serve immediately. Yield: 4 servings.

**Each Serving Provides:**

1 Bread

1 Fruit/Vegetable

50 Optional Calories

**Per Serving:**

183 Calories

34.9g Carbohydrate

0.8g Fat (0.1g saturated)

4.7g Fiber

10.6g Protein

2.5mg Cholesterol

250mg Sodium

56mg Calcium

2.9mg Iron

*tip*

*When you need a small amount of fresh lemon juice, go ahead and juice the whole lemon. Freeze the extra in ice cube trays, placing 1 tablespoon juice in each cube section.*

# Garden Macaroni and Cheese

Time: prep 20 minutes; cook 25 minutes

| Each Serving Provides: | |
| --- | --- |
| 2 Protein/Milk | |
| 2 Bread | |
| 60 Optional Calories | |

| Per Serving: | |
| --- | --- |
| 432 Calories | |
| 57.5g Carbohydrate | |
| 11.0g Fat (6.0g saturated) | |
| 3.4g Fiber | |
| 24.5g Protein | |
| 30mg Cholesterol | |
| 581mg Sodium | |
| 530mg Calcium | |
| 2.9mg Iron | |

½ cup dried shiitake mushrooms
½ cup hot water
8 ounces elbow macaroni, uncooked
1 cup frozen corn kernels, thawed
½ cup chopped green onions
½ cup chopped sweet red pepper
3 cups (1%) low-fat milk
¼ cup plus 2 tablespoons all-purpose flour
¼ teaspoon hot sauce
1½ cups (6 ounces) shredded reduced-fat Cheddar cheese
½ cup freshly grated Parmesan cheese
2 teaspoons dry mustard
¼ teaspoon salt
Vegetable cooking spray
3 tablespoons fine, dry breadcrumbs

## tip

*To chop green onions quickly, place 3 or 4 together on the cutting board, and chop them all at the same time.*

**1.** Combine mushrooms and hot water; let stand 15 minutes or until softened. Cook macaroni according to package directions, omitting salt and fat. Drain macaroni; place in a large bowl. Add corn, green onions, and red pepper, stirring to combine; set aside.

**2.** Combine milk and flour in a medium saucepan. Cook over medium heat 10 minutes or until thickened, stirring often. Stir in mushrooms, soaking liquid, and hot sauce. Add Cheddar cheese and next 3 ingredients, stirring well; cook, stirring often, until cheese melts and mixture is thoroughly heated. Remove from heat.

**3.** Pour mushroom-cheese sauce over macaroni mixture, stirring well. Spoon mixture into an 11- x 7- x 1½-inch baking dish coated with cooking spray. Sprinkle with breadcrumbs. Bake at 450° for 15 to 20 minutes or until bubbly. Yield: 6 servings.

Italian Beef and Noodles *(recipe, page 68)*

Caribbean Jerk Pork *(recipe, page 87)*; Garlic-Roasted Squash *(recipe, page 145)*

Sweet-and-Sour Pork *(recipe, page 88)*

# Tomato-Mushroom Pasta

**Time:** prep 5 minutes; cook 32 minutes

8       ounces angel hair pasta, uncooked
Vegetable cooking spray
2       teaspoons vegetable oil
1½    cups diced onion
½      cup diced sweet red pepper
2       cloves garlic, minced
2       cups sliced mushrooms
2       cups canned crushed tomatoes
¼      cup tomato paste
2       teaspoons Italian seasoning

**1.** Cook pasta according to package directions, omitting salt and fat. Drain, set aside, and keep warm.

**2.** Coat a medium skillet with cooking spray, and add oil; place over medium-high heat until hot. Add onion, pepper, and garlic; cook 2 minutes or until tender, stirring occasionally.

**3.** Add mushrooms and remaining 3 ingredients, and bring to a boil. Reduce heat, cover, and simmer 30 minutes, stirring occasionally.

**4.** Divide pasta evenly among 4 individual serving plates; spoon tomato-mushroom sauce evenly over pasta. Yield: 4 servings.

**Each Serving Provides:**

2 Bread
2 Fruit/Vegetable
1 Fat

**Per Serving:**

315 Calories
60.1g Carbohydrate
4.1g Fat (0.6g saturated)
4.7g Fiber
11.0g Protein
0mg Cholesterol
182mg Sodium
96mg Calcium
5.0mg Iron

*tip*

*To save time, you can substitute ½ teaspoon of minced garlic from a jar for each fresh clove.*

# Snow Pea and Pepper Salad *(photo, page 42)*

**Time:** prep 15 minutes; cook 10 minutes

**Each Serving Provides:**

1 Protein/Milk
1 Bread
1 Fruit/Vegetable
2 Fat
40 Optional Calories

**Per Serving:**

377 Calories
52.3g Carbohydrate
13.4g Fat (2.5g saturated)
3.5g Fiber
14.1g Protein
0mg Cholesterol
508mg Sodium
61mg Calcium
3.9mg Iron

| | |
|---|---|
| 6 | ounces angel hair pasta, uncooked |
| 1 | clove garlic, peeled |
| 2 | tablespoons plus 2 teaspoons low-sodium soy sauce, divided |
| 1 | tablespoon dark sesame oil, divided |
| ¾ | cup fresh cilantro |
| ¼ | cup plus 2 tablespoons reduced-fat creamy peanut butter |
| 3 | tablespoons lime juice |
| ½ | teaspoon hot sauce |
| ¼ | cup shredded carrot |
| ½ | cup chopped green onions |
| 2 | cups snow pea pods |
| ½ | cup thinly sliced sweet red pepper |
| 1 | tablespoon orange juice |
| 1 | clove garlic, minced |
| 2 | teaspoons rice vinegar |
| 1 | teaspoon peeled, minced gingerroot |

## ✎ *t i p*

*You can keep tightly wrapped fresh gingerroot in the freezer up to 2 months. There's no need to thaw before grating it for recipes.*

**1.** Cook pasta according to package directions, omitting salt and fat; drain well. Transfer pasta to a large bowl. Cover pasta, set aside, and keep warm.

**2.** Position knife blade in food processor bowl; add 1 clove garlic, 2 tablespoons low-sodium soy sauce, 2 teaspoons dark sesame oil, cilantro, peanut butter, lime juice, and hot sauce. Process mixture 1 minute. Add garlic mixture to pasta, tossing well to coat pasta. Add carrot and green onions to pasta; toss well. Set pasta mixture aside; cover and keep warm.

**3.** Wash snow peas; trim ends, and remove strings. Place snow peas in a medium bowl; cover with hot water, and let stand 1 minute. Drain. Add red pepper to snow peas; set aside.

**4.** Combine orange juice, remaining 2 teaspoons soy sauce, remaining 1 teaspoon sesame oil, minced garlic, vinegar, and gingerroot. Pour mixture over snow peas and pepper; toss well. Arrange snow pea mixture on 4 individual serving plates; top evenly with pasta mixture. Yield: 4 servings.

## Tips for Healthy Vegetarian Diets

With the recent emphasis on eating extra fruits, vegetables, and grains, more people have focused on the value of a vegetarian diet or have at least found new interest in eating a few meatless main dishes. For those on full-time vegetarian diets, the American Dietetic Association suggests the following guidelines:

• Eat a variety of fruits and vegetables, including good food sources for vitamin C like oranges, strawberries, and potatoes.

• Use low-fat milk and low-fat or nonfat versions of other dairy products.

• Limit your intake of low nutrient-dense foods like sweets and fatty foods.

• Select whole or unrefined grain products instead of refined, or use fortified or enriched cereal products.

• Limit the number of egg yolks you eat to three or four each week.

• Be sure you have a reliable source of vitamin $B_{12}$ if you're a vegan (someone who eats plant foods only). Good sources of this vitamin are fortified breakfast cereals, fortified soy beverages, or a daily vitamin $B_{12}$ supplement. If you have limited exposure to sunlight, then you also may need to take vitamin D supplements.

# Mushroom Fettuccine

**Time:** prep 10 minutes; cook 8 minutes

**Each Serving Provides:**

3 Bread
2 Fruit/Vegetable
1 Fat

**Per Serving:**

347 Calories
54.5g Carbohydrate
9.9g Fat (3.4g saturated)
2.9g Fiber
12.2g Protein
15mg Cholesterol
63mg Sodium
80mg Calcium
1.6mg Iron

*tip*

*Substitute the same amount of any long, thin noodle like spaghetti, linguine, or angel hair pasta for fettuccine.*

4    ounces fettuccine, uncooked
Vegetable cooking spray
1    teaspoon vegetable oil
1    cup chopped onion
2½   cups sliced fresh mushrooms
2    cloves garlic, minced
1    teaspoon dried basil
⅓    cup low-fat sour cream
Dash of freshly ground pepper

**1.** Cook pasta according to package directions, omitting salt and fat. Drain, set aside, and keep warm.

**2.** Coat a medium nonstick skillet with cooking spray, and add oil; place over medium-high heat until hot. Add onion, and cook 5 minutes or until tender, stirring often. Add mushrooms, garlic, and basil, and cook 2 additional minutes, stirring often. Remove from heat, and stir in sour cream and pepper.

**3.** Combine vegetable mixture and pasta; toss to coat. Serve immediately. Yield: 2 servings.

meats

# Italian Beef and Noodles *(photo, page 59)*

**Time:** prep 5 minutes; cook 35 minutes

Vegetable cooking spray

| | |
|---|---|
| 1 | pound ground round |
| 1 | cup sliced onion |
| 1 | cup diced sweet red pepper |
| 1 | teaspoon seeded, minced jalapeño pepper |
| 2 | cloves garlic, minced |
| ½ | cup no-salt-added tomato sauce |
| ½ | cup water |
| 2 | tablespoons no-salt-added tomato paste |
| 1 | teaspoon dried Italian seasoning |
| ½ | teaspoon salt |
| 2 | cups hot cooked medium egg noodles (cooked without salt or fat) |
| ¼ | cup low-fat sour cream |

Fresh basil sprigs (optional)

*✎ t i p*

*Use rubber gloves when handling jalapeños or other hot peppers. The fiery pepper pods can burn your skin.*

**1.** Coat a large nonstick skillet with cooking spray. Cook ground round in skillet over medium heat until browned, stirring until it crumbles; drain.

**2.** Add onion and next 3 ingredients. Cook, stirring constantly, 1 minute. Add tomato sauce and next 4 ingredients; bring to a boil. Cover, reduce heat, and simmer 30 minutes, stirring occasionally.

**3.** Arrange ½ cup noodles on each serving plate; top evenly with beef mixture. Top each serving with 1 tablespoon sour cream. Garnish with basil sprigs, if desired. Yield: 4 servings.

# Old-Fashioned Meat Loaf

**Time:** prep 10 minutes; cook 1 hour and 15 minutes

Vegetable cooking spray
1 teaspoon olive oil
1½ cups chopped fresh mushrooms
1 cup diced celery
1 cup chopped onion
1 clove garlic, minced
¾ pound ground round
¾ pound ground turkey
1 cup no-salt-added tomato sauce, divided
½ cup egg substitute
¾ cup soft breadcrumbs
¼ cup chopped fresh parsley
½ teaspoon dried basil
½ teaspoon pepper
¼ teaspoon salt

**Each Serving Provides:**

3 Protein/Milk

1 Bread

1 Fruit/Vegetable

**Per Serving:**

246 Calories

17.0g Carbohydrate

5.6g Fat (1.7g saturated)

2.3g Fiber

30.2g Protein

69mg Cholesterol

342mg Sodium

67mg Calcium

3.8mg Iron

**1.** Coat a large nonstick skillet with cooking spray, and add oil; place over medium-high heat until hot. Add mushrooms, celery, onion, and garlic; cook 5 to 10 minutes or until vegetables are tender, stirring often. (Add 1 to 2 tablespoons of water during cooking, if necessary.) Set mushroom mixture aside.

**2.** Combine ground round, turkey, ½ cup tomato sauce, and remaining 6 ingredients in a large bowl. Add mushroom mixture, stirring well. Press mixture into a 9- x 5- x 3-inch loafpan coated with cooking spray. Top evenly with remaining ½ cup tomato sauce.

**3.** Bake at 325° for 1 hour. Let stand in pan 10 to 15 minutes before slicing. Yield: 6 servings.

*tip*

*Process leftover or stale bread in the food processor; then freeze the crumbs in a heavy-duty, zip-top plastic freezer bag. Then you'll have breadcrumbs when you need them.*

# Quick Skillet Meat Loaf

**Time:** prep 5 minutes; cook 10 minutes

### Each Serving Provides:

3 Protein/Milk
40 Optional Calories

### Per Serving:

158 Calories
3.8g Carbohydrate
5.6g Fat (2.6g saturated)
0.6g Fiber
22.1g Protein
51mg Cholesterol
126mg Sodium
104mg Calcium
1.9mg Iron

*✎ tip*

*You can use 1 whole egg for every ¼ cup of egg substitute.*

Vegetable cooking spray
½    cup finely chopped onion
1    clove garlic, minced
½    teaspoon dried oregano
½    teaspoon freshly ground pepper
1    pound ground round
¼    cup egg substitute
¾    cup (3 ounces) shredded part-skim mozzarella cheese
½    cup no-salt-added tomato sauce

**1.** Coat an 8-inch nonstick skillet with cooking spray; place over medium heat until hot. Add onion and garlic; cook 3 minutes or until tender, stirring often. Stir in oregano and pepper. Transfer onion mixture to a large bowl.

**2.** Wipe skillet with a paper towel; coat bottom of skillet with cooking spray. Add ground round and egg substitute to onion mixture; mix well and divide in half. Place half of meat mixture in skillet, and pat lightly to spread mixture evenly over bottom of skillet. Sprinkle evenly with cheese. Pat remaining meat mixture evenly over cheese.

**3.** Place skillet over high heat; cook 3 to 4 minutes or until bottom of meat mixture is browned. Cut into 6 wedges. Turn each wedge over carefully, and cook 3 to 4 additional minutes or until meat is browned and cheese is melted. Pour tomato sauce over meat; cover and cook 1 additional minute. Serve immediately. Yield: 6 servings.

# Beef Curry

**Time:** prep 10 minutes; cook 1 hour and 45 minutes

| | |
|---|---|
| 1½ | pounds lean boneless round steak, cut into 1-inch pieces |
| 1 | cup sliced onion |
| 1 | cup water |
| 1 | small apple, peeled, cored, and chopped |
| ¼ | cup no-salt-added tomato paste |
| 1 | tablespoon brown sugar |
| 1 | tablespoon curry powder |
| 1 | tablespoon low-sodium soy sauce |
| 1 | teaspoon peeled, grated gingerroot |
| 1 | teaspoon beef-flavored bouillon granules |
| ½ | teaspoon chili powder |
| 2 | cloves garlic, minced |
| 2 | tablespoons water |
| 2 | teaspoons cornstarch |
| 1 | (15¼-ounce) can pineapple chunks in juice, drained |
| 6 | cups hot cooked rice (cooked without salt or fat) |

**Each Serving Provides:**

3 Protein/Milk

2 Bread

1 Fruit/Vegetable

**Per Serving:**

440 Calories

65.0g Carbohydrate

5.0g Fat (1.7g saturated)

2.5g Fiber

30.8g Protein

65mg Cholesterol

285mg Sodium

46mg Calcium

4.9mg Iron

**1.** Combine first 12 ingredients in a 2-quart casserole. Cover and bake at 350° for 1 hour and 30 minutes or until steak is tender.

**2.** Combine 2 tablespoons water and cornstarch; stir to dissolve cornstarch. Add cornstarch mixture to beef mixture; stirring well. Stir in pineapple. Cover casserole, and bake 15 additional minutes or until sauce is thickened.

**3.** Arrange 1 cup rice on each of 6 individual serving plates; spoon beef mixture evenly over rice. Yield: 6 servings.

### tip

*Refrigerate leftover tomato paste in an air-tight non-metallic container. You can add it to soups, stews, or casseroles for extra flavor.*

# Oriental Beef

Time: prep 8 minutes; cook 51 minutes

Vegetable cooking spray
| | |
|---|---|
| 1 | cup sliced onion |
| 1 | clove garlic, minced |
| 1 | cup unsweetened pineapple juice |
| ¼ | cup no-salt-added tomato paste |
| 2 | tablespoons brown sugar |
| 2 | tablespoons low-sodium soy sauce |
| 1 | tablespoon red wine vinegar |
| 2 | teaspoons curry powder |
| 1 | tablespoon plus 1 teaspoon all-purpose flour |
| 1½ | pounds lean boneless round steak, cut into 1-inch pieces |
| 1 | teaspoon vegetable oil |
| ¾ | cup drained canned sliced water chestnuts |
| ½ | medium-size green pepper, cut into strips |
| ½ | medium-size sweet red pepper, cut into strips |
| 8 | strips lemon rind |
| 6 | cups hot cooked rice (cooked without salt or fat) |

## ✍ *t i p*

*Use a vegetable peeler to cut lemon rind into thin strips.*

**1.** Coat a wok or large nonstick skillet with cooking spray. Place over medium-high heat until hot. Add onion and garlic, and stir-fry 3 minutes or until tender; transfer to a medium bowl. Add pineapple juice and next 5 ingredients to onion mixture; set aside.

**2.** Sprinkle flour over steak, tossing to coat well.

**3.** Drizzle oil around top of wok, coating sides. Add steak pieces; stir-fry 3 minutes or until meat is browned on all sides. Add pineapple juice mixture, and bring to a boil. Reduce heat to low; cover and simmer 30 minutes.

**4.** Add water chestnuts, pepper strips, and lemon rind to beef mixture, stirring to combine; cover and cook 15 additional minutes or until meat is tender. Remove and discard rind before serving.

**5.** Arrange 1 cup rice on each of 6 individual serving plates. Top with beef and vegetable mixture: Yield: 6 servings.

## Look for the Lean Meats

The leanest cuts of red meat have more muscle than fat. Higher-fat cuts have more marbling, or flecks of fat. The leanest cuts of meat are listed below:

- Beef: top round, top sirloin steak, tenderloin, eye of round, and round tip
- Veal: top round, leg cutlet, arm steak, sirloin steak, loin chop, and rib chop
- Lamb: leg of lamb, shank, sirloin roast, and loin chop
- Pork: tenderloin, loin chop, top loin roast, Canadian bacon, and lean cured ham

# Beef Stir-Fry with Port Prunes

**Time:** prep 18 minutes; cook 6 minutes

**Each Serving Provides:**

3 Protein/Milk

2 Bread

2 Fruit/Vegetable

1 Fat

**Per Serving:**

502 Calories

71.1g Carbohydrate

7.6g Fat (2.1g saturated)

3.9g Fiber

31.8g Protein

65mg Cholesterol

141mg Sodium

58mg Calcium

5.1mg Iron

| | |
|---|---|
| 4 | large pitted prunes, halved |
| ¼ | cup water |
| 2 | tablespoons port wine |
| 1 | teaspoon low-sodium soy sauce |
| ¼ | teaspoon grated orange rind |

Vegetable cooking spray

| | |
|---|---|
| 1 | medium zucchini, cut into very thin strips |
| 1 | medium carrot, cut into very thin strips |
| 1 | teaspoon vegetable oil |
| ½ | pound lean boneless round steak, sliced diagonally across grain into thin strips |
| ¼ | cup unsweetened orange juice |
| 1 | teaspoon cornstarch |
| 2 | cups hot cooked rice (cooked without salt or fat) |

**1.** Combine first 5 ingredients in a small bowl; let stand 10 minutes to plump prunes.

**2.** Coat a wok or large nonstick skillet with cooking spray; place over medium-high heat until hot. Add zucchini and carrot, and stir-fry 30 seconds or until crisp-tender. Transfer vegetables to a bowl.

**3.** Drizzle oil around top of wok, coating sides; add beef, and stir-fry 2 minutes or until browned. Return zucchini mixture to wok, and stir in prune mixture; stir-fry 2 minutes.

**4.** Combine orange juice and cornstarch, stirring until cornstarch is dissolved; add to beef mixture. Cook, stirring constantly, 1 to 2 minutes, until mixture is thickened.

## ✿ tip

*It's easier to cut thin slices from partially frozen steak. Just place the steak in the freezer for about 15 minutes before slicing it.*

**5.** Arrange 1 cup rice on each of 2 individual serving plates; spoon beef mixture evenly over rice. Yield: 2 servings.

*Note:* For more flavor, allow the prune-wine mixture to marinate up to 8 hours in the refrigerator.

## How to Cook Meat the Low-Fat Way

Prepare and cook meat using low-fat techniques to keep fat content to a minimum.

- Trim away any visible fat from the meat before you cook it.
- Reduce or omit oil from marinade recipes.
- Flavor meats with herbs, spices, seasoning blends, citrus juices, wine, or flavored vinegars; none of these ingredients add fat.

- Roast, broil, or grill meat to allow the fat to drip away as the meat cooks.
- Brown ground beef in a nonstick skillet coated with cooking spray or with no added fat.
- Place browned ground beef into a colander to drain excess fat.

# Beef Satay

Time: prep 5 minutes; marinate 2 hours; cook 9 minutes

**Each Serving Provides:**
3 Protein/Milk
1 Bread

**Per Serving:**
264 Calories
28.1g Carbohydrate
6.2g Fat (1.7g saturated)
0.5g Fiber
22.1g Protein
49mg Cholesterol
296mg Sodium
15mg Calcium
2.6mg Iron

✿ *t i p*

*If you rinse your measuring cup with very hot water before using it to measure peanut butter, the peanut butter won't stick to the cup.*

¾  cup water
1   tablespoon low-sodium soy sauce
1   teaspoon beef-flavored bouillon granules
1   teaspoon peeled, minced gingerroot
1   clove garlic, minced
1   pound lean boneless round steak, cut into thin strips
Vegetable cooking spray
1   tablespoon water
2   teaspoons cornstarch
⅓  cup reduced-fat creamy peanut butter
3   cups hot cooked rice (cooked without salt or fat)

**1.** Combine first 5 ingredients in a large heavy-duty, zip-top plastic bag. Add steak; seal bag, and turn bag to coat steak. Marinate in refrigerator at least 2 hours, turning bag occasionally.

**2.** Remove steak from marinade, reserving marinade. Place marinade in a small saucepan; bring to a boil. Remove from heat, and set aside.

**3.** Thread steak evenly onto twelve 8-inch skewers. Arrange skewers on rack of a broiler pan coated with cooking spray. Broil 5½ inches from heat (with electric oven door partially opened) 7 to 8 minutes or to desired degree of doneness, basting frequently with reserved soy sauce marinade.

**4.** Combine water and cornstarch, stirring until cornstarch dissolves. Add cornstarch mixture and peanut butter to remaining marinade; place saucepan over medium-high heat. Bring to a boil, and cook, stirring constantly, 1 minute. Arrange ½ cup rice on each of 6 individual serving plates. Place 2 skewers on each serving; top evenly with thickened marinade. Yield: 6 servings.

# Marinated Steak

**Time:** prep 5 minutes; marinate 2 hours; cook 23 minutes

| | |
|---|---|
| 1 | (1-pound) lean boneless top sirloin steak (1½ inches thick) |
| ½ | cup dry red wine |
| ¼ | cup canned no-salt-added beef broth, undiluted |
| 2 | tablespoons low-sodium soy sauce |
| 2 | tablespoons barbecue sauce |
| 2 | tablespoons prepared mustard |
| ¼ | teaspoon freshly ground pepper |
| 1 | clove garlic, minced |

Vegetable cooking spray

**Each Serving Provides:**
3 Protein/Milk

**Per Serving:**
213 Calories
3.0g Carbohydrate
7.0g Fat (2.5g saturated)
0.2g Fiber
27.9g Protein
79mg Cholesterol
465mg Sodium
23mg Calcium
3.5mg Iron

**1.** Trim fat from steak. Combine wine and next 6 ingredients in a large heavy-duty, zip-top plastic bag. Add steak; seal bag, and turn bag to coat steak. Marinate in refrigerator at least 2 hours, turning bag occasionally.

**2.** Remove steak from marinade, reserving marinade. Place marinade in a small saucepan; bring to a boil. Remove from heat, and set aside.

**3.** Place steak on rack of a broiler pan coated with cooking spray. Broil 5½ inches from heat (with electric oven door partially opened) 8 minutes on each side or to desired degree of doneness, basting frequently with reserved marinade. Let steak stand 5 minutes. Cut diagonally across grain into thin slices. Serve with remaining marinade. Yield: 4 servings.

*tip*

*To grill the steaks instead of broiling them, cook covered over hot coals for 5 to 6 minutes on each side.*

# Veal with Mushroom Sauce

**Time:** prep 8 minutes; cook 11 minutes

| | |
|---|---|
| 6 | ounces spinach fettuccine, uncooked |
| | Vegetable cooking spray |
| 2 | teaspoons vegetable oil |
| 1 | pound veal cutlets, cut into ½-inch strips |
| 3 | cups sliced fresh mushrooms |
| 1 | medium onion, finely chopped |
| 1 | clove garlic, minced |
| 2 | tablespoons brandy |
| 1 | cup skim milk |
| 1 | teaspoon Dijon mustard |
| 1 | teaspoon chicken-flavored bouillon granules |
| 2 | tablespoons water |
| 2 | teaspoons cornstarch |
| 3 | tablespoons low-fat sour cream |

### ✿ t i p

*Use an egg slicer to slice mushrooms quickly.*

**1.** Prepare pasta according to package directions, omitting salt and fat; drain. Set aside, and keep warm.

**2.** Coat a large skillet with cooking spray, and add oil; place skillet over medium-high heat until hot. Add veal, and cook 5 minutes or until browned, stirring often. Transfer veal to a plate; set aside.

**3.** Add mushrooms, onion, and garlic to skillet; cook over medium-high heat 3 minutes or until vegetables are tender, stirring often. Add brandy, and cook 2 minutes. Add milk, mustard, and bouillon granules to vegetable mixture. Combine water and cornstarch, stirring until cornstarch dissolves; add to vegetable mixture. Bring to a boil, and cook, stirring constantly, 1 minute. Remove from heat and stir in sour cream. Return veal to skillet, and cook until thoroughly heated. Arrange pasta on a platter; top with veal mixture. Yield: 4 servings.

Chicken Quesadillas *(recipe, page 92)*

79

Grilled Dijon Chicken (*recipe, page 103*)

# Lemon Lamb Chops

**Time:** prep 5 minutes; marinate 2 hours; cook 10 minutes

| | |
|---|---|
| 8 | (3-ounce) lean lamb loin chops (1 inch thick) |
| 1 | teaspoon grated lemon rind |
| 3 | tablespoons fresh lemon juice |
| 1 | tablespoon chopped fresh rosemary |
| 2 | teaspoons chopped fresh mint |
| ¼ | teaspoon salt |

Vegetable cooking spray

**1.** Trim fat from chops. Combine lemon rind and next 4 ingredients in a large heavy-duty, zip-top plastic bag. Add chops; seal bag, and turn bag to coat chops. Marinate in refrigerator 2 hours, turning bag occasionally.

**2.** Remove chops from marinade, discarding marinade. Place chops on rack of a broiler pan coated with cooking spray. Broil 5½ inches from heat (with electric oven door partially opened) 5 minutes on each side or to desired degree of doneness. Yield: 4 servings.

**Each Serving Provides:**

3 Protein/Milk

**Per Serving:**

212 Calories
1.2g Carbohydrate
9.5g Fat (3.3g saturated)
0.0g Fiber
28.8g Protein
91mg Cholesterol
228mg Sodium
23mg Calcium
2.0mg Iron

*tip*

*Grate the whole lemon rind, and freeze any extra to have on hand for other recipes.*

# Pork with Apricot Sauce

**Time:** prep 5 minutes; cook 12 minutes

2    (4-ounce) boneless lean pork loin chops
¼    teaspoon freshly ground pepper
Dash of paprika
Vegetable cooking spray
½    cup finely chopped green onions
⅔    cup apricot nectar
½    teaspoon beef-flavored bouillon granules
2    tablespoons water
2    teaspoons cornstarch

**1.** Sprinkle both sides of chops with pepper and paprika. Place pork on rack of a broiler pan coated with cooking spray. Broil 5½ inches from heat (with electric oven door partially opened) 5 minutes on each side or to desired degree of doneness. Transfer chops to a serving platter; set aside, and keep warm.

**2.** Coat a medium skillet with cooking spray; place skillet over medium-high heat until hot. Add green onions and cook 1 minute or until tender, stirring often. Add apricot nectar and bouillon granules.

**3.** Combine water and cornstarch, stirring until cornstarch dissolves; add to skillet. Bring to a boil; reduce heat, and cook, stirring constantly, 1 minute or until thickened. Pour apricot mixture over pork. Yield: 2 servings.

*tip*

*Use 2 green onions to get about ½ cup of chopped green onions.*

# Tangy Hoisin Pork

**Time:** prep 5 minutes; marinate 1 hour; cook 35 minutes

2   green onions, finely chopped
1   tablespoon plus 1 teaspoon hoisin sauce
1   tablespoon low-sodium soy sauce
2   teaspoons dry sherry
1   teaspoon peeled, grated gingerroot
6   (4-ounce) boneless lean pork loin chops
Vegetable cooking spray

**1.** Combine first 5 ingredients in a large heavy-duty, zip-top plastic bag. Add pork; seal bag, and turn bag to coat pork. Marinate in refrigerator 1 hour.

**2.** Remove pork from marinade, and place in a 13- x 9- x 2-inch baking dish coated with cooking spray; pour marinade over pork. Bake at 350° for 35 minutes or until pork is done. Yield: 6 servings.

**Each Serving Provides:**
3 Protein/Milk

**Per Serving:**
186 Calories
1.3g Carbohydrate
8.7g Fat (3.0g saturated)
0.2g Fiber
23.6g Protein
68mg Cholesterol
178mg Sodium
12mg Calcium
1.1mg Iron

*tip*

*If you don't have dry sherry on hand, substitute ½ teaspoon vanilla extract for 2 teaspoons of sherry.*

# Italian Pork Chops and Rice

**Time:** prep 5 minutes; cook 1 hour and 17 minutes

**Each Serving Provides:**

3 Protein/Milk

1 Bread

1 Fruit/Vegetable

**Per Serving:**

377 Calories

39.1g Carbohydrate

11.7g Fat (3.8g saturated)

2.2g Fiber

27.7g Protein

74mg Cholesterol

90mg Sodium

89mg Calcium

4.0mg Iron

Vegetable cooking spray

4      (4-ounce) boneless lean pork loin chops

1      medium onion, thickly sliced

1      cup diced green pepper

⅔     cup long-grain rice, uncooked

2      (14½-ounce) cans no-salt-added Italian-style stewed tomatoes, undrained

1      teaspoon Italian seasoning

⅛     teaspoon freshly ground pepper

**1.** Coat a medium nonstick skillet with cooking spray; place over medium-high heat until hot. Add pork chops, and cook 1 to 2 minutes on each side or just until browned.

**2.** Transfer pork chops to an 11- x 7- x 1½-inch baking dish coated with cooking spray; top with onion, green pepper, and rice. Pour tomatoes over pork; sprinkle with Italian seasoning and pepper. Cover and bake at 350° for 1 hour and 15 minutes or until pork is tender. Yield: 4 servings.

# Honey-Pecan Pork

**Time:** prep 5 minutes; cook 11 minutes

4     (4-ounce) boneless lean pork loin chops
3     tablespoons all-purpose flour
Vegetable cooking spray
1     teaspoon vegetable oil
½     cup water, divided
2     teaspoons cornstarch
3     tablespoons dry sherry
2     tablespoons hoisin sauce
1     tablespoon honey
1     tablespoon coarsely chopped pecans

**Each Serving Provides:**

3 Protein/Milk
1 Fat

**Per Serving:**

264 Calories
12.7g Carbohydrate
11.1g Fat (3.3g saturated)
0.4g Fiber
24.4g Protein
68mg Cholesterol
163mg Sodium
12mg Calcium
1.4mg Iron

**1.** Combine pork chops and flour in a large heavy-duty, zip-top plastic bag. Seal bag, and turn bag to coat pork.

**2.** Coat a medium nonstick skillet with cooking spray, and add oil; place over medium-high heat until hot. Add pork and any flour remaining in the bag. Cook 4 minutes on each side. Transfer pork to a plate; set aside, and keep warm.

**3.** Combine ¼ cup water and cornstarch in a 1-cup liquid measuring cup, stirring until cornstarch dissolves. Add remaining ¼ cup water, sherry, hoisin sauce, and honey; stir to combine. Add cornstarch mixture to skillet, bring to a boil; reduce heat, and cook, stirring constantly, 1 minute or until thickened.

**4.** Return pork to skillet; turn chops to coat both sides with sherry mixture. Sprinkle with pecans. Cover and cook 2 to 3 minutes or until pork is thoroughly heated. Yield: 4 servings.

*tip*

*Wrap the cooked pork in foil, and place it in the oven on the lowest temperature to keep it warm while you make the sauce.*

# Pork Scaloppine

**Time:** prep 5 minutes; cook 13 minutes

Each Serving Provides:
3 Protein/Milk
50 Optional Calories

Per Serving:
242 Calories
7.1g Carbohydrate
11.3g Fat (4.0g saturated)
0.7g Fiber
25.0g Protein
72mg Cholesterol
151mg Sodium
31mg Calcium
1.7mg Iron

| | |
|---|---|
| 3 | tablespoons all-purpose flour |
| ⅛ | teaspoon salt |
| ⅛ | teaspoon freshly ground pepper |
| 4 | (4-ounce) boneless lean pork loin chops |

Vegetable cooking spray

| | |
|---|---|
| 1 | teaspoon vegetable oil |
| 1 | cup whole fresh mushrooms |
| 4 | green onions, finely chopped |
| ¼ | cup white wine |
| ½ | cup canned no-salt-added chicken broth, undiluted |
| 3 | tablespoons low-fat sour cream |

**1.** Combine flour, salt, and pepper in a shallow dish; dredge pork chops in flour mixture.

**2.** Coat a medium nonstick skillet with cooking spray, and add oil; place skillet over medium-high heat until hot. Add pork, and cook 3 to 4 minutes on each side. Transfer pork to a plate; set aside, and keep warm.

**3.** Add mushrooms and green onions to skillet, and cook 3 minutes or until tender, stirring often. Stir in wine and broth; cook until liquid is reduced by half, stirring often.

**4.** Return pork to skillet; cover and cook 2 to 3 minutes or until thoroughly heated. Remove from heat and stir in sour cream.
Yield: 4 servings.

## tip

*For a no-cleanup way to dredge the pork chops in flour, place the flour, salt, pepper, and pork in a zip-top plastic bag. Then seal the bag, and shake until the meat is coated.*

# Caribbean Jerk Pork *(photo, pages 60 and 61)*

**Time:** prep 5 minutes; marinate 8 hours; cook 1 hour and 40 minutes

| | |
|---|---|
| 1 | (4-pound) lean boneless pork loin roast |
| ¼ | cup fresh lime juice |
| ¼ | cup fresh orange juice |
| 2 | tablespoons dark brown sugar |
| 1 | teaspoon onion powder |
| 1 | teaspoon ground allspice |
| 1 | teaspoon dried thyme |
| 1 | teaspoon ground red pepper |
| ½ | teaspoon ground cinnamon |
| 1 | medium clove garlic, minced |

Vegetable cooking spray

**1.** Trim fat from pork roast. Place pork in a large heavy-duty, zip-top plastic bag. Combine lime juice, orange juice, and next 7 ingredients; pour over pork. Seal bag; turn bag to coat pork. Marinate in refrigerator 8 hours, turning bag occasionally.

**2.** Line a large roasting pan with aluminum foil, and coat with cooking spray. Remove pork from marinade, reserving marinade, and place pork in prepared pan. Insert a meat thermometer in thickest part of pork, if desired. Spoon reserved marinade evenly over pork. Bake, uncovered, at 350° for 1 hour and 30 minutes or until thermometer registers 160°, basting occasionally with juices. Cover with aluminum foil, and let stand 10 minutes before slicing. Yield: 16 servings.

**Each Serving Provides:**

3 Protein/Milk

**Per Serving:**

138 Calories
2.9g Carbohydrate
2.9g Fat (1.0g saturated)
0.1g Fiber
23.9g Protein
74mg Cholesterol
57mg Sodium
14mg Calcium
1.7mg Iron

*✒ t i p*

*You'll get more fresh juice from oranges, lemons, and limes if you let them come to room temperature before juicing. Or, microwave cold citrus fruit at HIGH for 10 seconds before juicing.*

# Sweet-and-Sour Pork (photo, page 62)

**Time:** prep 15 minutes; cook 7 minutes

**Each Serving Provides:**

3 Protein/Milk

2 Bread

2 Fruit/Vegetable

40 Optional Calories

**Per Serving:**

470 Calories

75.7g Carbohydrate

4.6g Fat (1.2g saturated)

4.3g Fiber

30.9g Protein

74mg Cholesterol

323mg Sodium

131mg Calcium

4.9mg Iron

Vegetable cooking spray

1    teaspoon peanut oil

1    pound lean boneless pork loin, cut into 1-inch cubes

1    cup diagonally sliced celery

1    medium onion, cut into wedges

½    medium-size green pepper, seeded and cut into 1-inch pieces

1    clove garlic, minced

2    (14½-ounce) cans no-salt-added whole tomatoes, drained and
     halved

1    (8-ounce) can pineapple chunks in juice, drained

¾    cup water, divided

1    tablespoon cornstarch

3    tablespoons ketchup

2    tablespoons red wine vinegar

1    tablespoon brown sugar

2    teaspoons low-sodium soy sauce

4    cups hot cooked rice (cooked without salt or fat)

*✐ t i p*

*If you don't have red wine vinegar, you can substitute cider vinegar.*

**1.** Coat a wok or large nonstick skillet with cooking spray; drizzle oil around top of wok, coating sides. Heat wok at medium-high (375°) until hot. Add pork; stir-fry 3 minutes or until browned. Remove pork from wok; set aside, and keep warm. Add celery, onion, pepper, and garlic to wok; stir-fry 2 to 3 minutes or until crisp-tender. Add tomato and pineapple; stir-fry 1 minute.

**2.** Combine 2 tablespoons of water and cornstarch in a 2-cup liquid measuring cup, stirring until cornstarch dissolves. Add remaining water and next 4 ingredients, stirring well. Return pork to wok. Add cornstarch mixture to wok. Bring to a boil, and cook, stirring constantly, 1 minute or until thickened. Arrange 1 cup rice on each of 4 individual serving plates; top evenly with pork mixture. Yield: 4 servings.

poultry

# Saucy Chicken Casserole

**Time:** prep 10 minutes; cook 31 minutes

**Each Serving Provides:**

3 Protein/Milk

1 Fruit/Vegetable

1 Fat

**Per Serving:**

254 Calories

13.6g Carbohydrate

8.1g Fat (2.0g saturated)

1.4g Fiber

30.6g Protein

74mg Cholesterol

298mg Sodium

138mg Calcium

1.8mg Iron

Vegetable cooking spray

| | |
|---|---|
| 1 | teaspoon vegetable oil |
| 1 | cup finely chopped onion |
| 1 | clove garlic, minced |
| 1 | (15-ounce) can no-salt-added crushed tomatoes, undrained |
| ¼ | teaspoon dried marjoram |
| ¼ | teaspoon dried oregano |
| 3 | cups chopped cooked chicken breast (skinned before cooking and cooked without salt and fat) |
| 1 | tablespoon margarine |
| 1 | tablespoon all-purpose flour |
| ¾ | cup skim milk |
| ¼ | teaspoon dry mustard |
| 1 | tablespoon Parmesan cheese |
| 1 | tablespoon fine, dry breadcrumbs |

*✒ tip*

*You'll get 3 cups of chopped cooked chicken from 1 pound of uncooked skinned, boned chicken breasts.*

**1.** Coat a medium saucepan with cooking spray, and add oil; place over medium-high heat until hot. Add onion and garlic; cook, stirring constantly, until onion is tender. Add tomato, marjoram, and oregano; bring to a boil. Reduce heat; simmer 10 minutes. Stir in chicken; set aside.

**2.** Melt margarine in a small heavy saucepan over medium heat; add flour. Cook, stirring constantly with a wire whisk, 1 minute. Gradually add milk, stirring constantly, and cook 5 minutes or until thickened and bubbly. Remove from heat; stir in mustard. Add to chicken mixture, stirring to combine. Spoon mixture into a 2-quart casserole dish coated with cooking spray.

**3.** Combine cheese and breadcrumbs; sprinkle evenly over chicken mixture. Bake at 350° for 20 minutes. Yield: 4 servings.

# Spicy Chicken Tacos

**Time:** prep 5 minutes; cook 10 minutes

| | |
|---|---|
| 8 | taco shells |
| 1½ | cups chopped cooked chicken breast (skinned before cooking and cooked without salt and fat) |
| ½ | cup no-salt-added tomato sauce |
| ½ | teaspoon ground cumin |
| ¼ | teaspoon dried crushed red pepper |
| 2 | cloves garlic, minced |
| 8 | green leaf lettuce leaves |
| 1 | medium tomato, seeded and diced |
| ½ | cup nonfat sour cream |
| 1 | tablespoon chopped green onions |

**1.** Place taco shells on an ungreased baking sheet. Bake at 350° for 5 minutes or until thoroughly heated.

**2.** Combine chicken, tomato sauce, cumin, red pepper, and garlic in a medium saucepan; cook over low heat 5 minutes or until thoroughly heated, stirring often.

**3.** Place 1 lettuce leaf in each shell. Place ¼ cup chicken mixture in each shell. Top chicken mixture evenly with tomato and sour cream; sprinkle with green onions. Yield: 4 servings (2 tacos per serving).

**Each Serving Provides:**

2 Protein/Milk

1 Bread

1 Fruit/Vegetable

40 Optional Calories

**Per Serving:**

252 Calories

19.2g Carbohydrate

8.9g Fat (1.6g saturated)

2.6g Fiber

22.1g Protein

48mg Cholesterol

162mg Sodium

25mg Calcium

1.1mg Iron

*tip*

*Freeze leftover tomato sauce in sections of an ice cube tray; then pop out the cubes to store in a heavy-duty, zip-top plastic bag in the freezer.*

# Chicken Quesadillas *(photo, page 79)*

**Time:** prep 5 minutes; cook 6 minutes

**Each Serving Provides:**
2 Protein/Milk
2 Bread
1 Fruit/Vegetable

**Per Serving:**
Per Serving:
241 Calories
26.9g Carbohydrate
6.1g Fat (2.0g saturated)
3.0g Fiber
20.5g Protein
43mg Cholesterol
476mg Sodium
154mg Calcium
2.1mg Iron

| | |
|---|---|
| 1 | cup frozen whole-kernel corn, thawed |
| ½ | cup diced green pepper |
| ½ | cup seeded, diced tomato |
| 2 | tablespoons minced fresh cilantro |
| 2 | teaspoons balsamic vinegar |
| ¼ | teaspoon salt |
| 1 | cup chopped cooked chicken breast (skinned before cooking and cooked without salt and fat) |
| ½ | cup thick and chunky hot salsa |
| 6 | (6-inch) flour tortillas |
| ¼ | cup plus 2 tablespoons (1½ ounces) shredded reduced-fat sharp Cheddar cheese |

Vegetable cooking spray
Shredded lettuce (optional)

**1.** Combine first 6 ingredients; stir well, and set aside.

**2.** Combine chicken and hot salsa in a small bowl; arrange mixture evenly over 3 tortillas. Sprinkle evenly with cheese, and top with remaining tortillas.

**3.** Coat a medium nonstick skillet with cooking spray; place over medium-high heat until hot. Place one quesadilla in skillet. Cook 1 minute on each side or until golden. Repeat procedure with remaining quesadillas. Cut each quesadilla into 4 wedges. Arrange shredded lettuce on each of 4 individual serving plates, if desired. Place 3 quesadilla wedges over lettuce on each plate. Serve with corn salsa. Yield: 4 servings (3 quesadilla wedges and ½ cup corn salsa per serving).

## ✎ *t i p*

*To seed tomatoes easily, cut them in half horizontally, and squeeze each half in your palm to remove the seeds.*

# Southwestern Chicken Pasta *(cover photo)*

**Time:** prep 10 minutes; cook 10 minutes

Olive-oil flavored vegetable cooking spray
¾      pound skinned, boned chicken breasts, cut into thin strips
2½    cups sliced fresh mushrooms
2       medium-size sweet red peppers, seeded and cut into strips
2       medium-size sweet yellow peppers, seeded and cut into strips
2       cloves garlic, minced
1       jalapeño pepper, seeded and finely chopped
3       tablespoons dry white wine
½      cup canned low-sodium chicken broth, undiluted
1       tablespoon olive oil
4½    cups hot cooked penne (short tubular pasta), cooked without
        salt or fat
¼      cup diagonally sliced green onions
¼      cup chopped fresh cilantro
¼      cup freshly grated Parmesan cheese
¼      teaspoon salt
⅛      teaspoon freshly ground pepper
Fresh cilantro sprigs (optional)

**1.** Coat a large nonstick skillet with cooking spray; place skillet over medium-high heat until hot. Add chicken and next 5 ingredients; cook, stirring constantly, 4 minutes or until chicken is lightly browned. Add wine, and cook, stirring constantly, 2 minutes or until wine evaporates. Add chicken broth; reduce heat to medium, and simmer, uncovered, 2 minutes. Remove chicken mixture from heat; set aside.

**2.** Add olive oil to pasta, and toss well. Add chicken mixture, and stir well. Add green onions and next 4 ingredients, tossing gently to combine. Arrange mixture on individual serving plates; garnish with cilantro sprigs, if desired. Yield: 6 servings.

**Each Serving Provides:**

1 Protein/Milk

1 Bread

1 Fruit/Vegetable

1 Fat

50 Optional Calories

**Per Serving:**

240 Calories

26.6g Carbohydrate

5.3g Fat (1.4g saturated)

2.2g Fiber

20.1g Protein

36mg Cholesterol

229mg Sodium

81mg Calcium

2.9mg Iron

*✑ t i p*

*Cilantro adds the characteristic southwestern flavor to this recipe. You can substitute fresh parsley and the flavor will be good, but not the same.*

# Turkey Sausage Lasagna

**Time:** prep 22 minutes; cook 1 hour and 16 minutes

Vegetable cooking spray
¼   pound turkey Italian sausage, casings removed
1   cup chopped green pepper
½   cup chopped onion
¼   teaspoon fennel seeds, crushed
1   teaspoon dried oregano, divided
1   (15-ounce) can no-salt-added crushed tomatoes, undrained
¼   teaspoon salt
6   lasagna noodles
1   cup part-skim ricotta cheese
½   cup (2 ounces) shredded part-skim mozzarella cheese
¼   cup egg substitute
¼   cup freshly grated Parmesan cheese
⅛   teaspoon dried crushed red pepper

### tip

*Using a sharp knife, split sausage casings; then carefully peel away the casings and discard them.*

**1.** Coat a large nonstick skillet with cooking spray; place over medium-high heat until hot. Add sausage, chopped pepper, onion, fennel seeds, and ½ teaspoon oregano; cook 5 minutes or until vegetables are tender and sausage is browned, stirring until sausage crumbles. Add tomato and salt, stirring well. Bring to a boil; reduce heat, and simmer, uncovered, 20 minutes.

**2.** Cook pasta according to package directions, omitting salt and fat; drain. Set aside and keep warm.

**3.** Combine remaining ½ teaspoon oregano, ricotta cheese, and remaining ingredients in a medium bowl, stirring well. Spread ricotta mixture evenly over noodles; roll noodles up jellyroll fashion beginning at narrow end.

**4.** Spread ½ cup tomato sauce mixture in an 8-inch square baking dish coated with cooking spray. Place lasagna rolls, seam sides down, on sauce. Spoon remaining sauce over rolls.

**5.** Bake, covered, at 350° for 40 minutes or until thoroughly heated. Let stand 10 minutes before serving. Yield: 6 servings.

## *Safe Ways to Sidestep Salmonella*

Take just a few precautions when you handle raw chicken or turkey, and you won't have to worry about salmonella (the bacteria which causes flu-like symptoms) that may be present in uncooked poultry.

*Handling and Storage*
• Make sure that uncooked poultry is bagged separately from other food at the supermarket.
• Do not leave uncooked poultry at room temperature for any length of time.
• Use a clean knife and cutting board to prepare chicken; then wash your hands, the knife, and the cutting board in hot, soapy water to prevent contaminating other foods.
• Keep poultry in the refrigerator only one to two days. Most cooked poultry will keep in the refrigerator for up to four days; keep cooked ground chicken and chicken in gravy only one or two days after cooking it.
• Don't leave cooked poultry at room temperature for longer than 2 hours.
• Never place cooked chicken or turkey in an unwashed container that has held uncooked poultry.

*Thawing*
• The best place to thaw chicken is in the refrigerator. To thaw it quickly, place the wrapped package in a bowl of cold water, and allow it to sit at room temperature for 30 minutes. Change the water, and then repeat the process just until the chicken is thawed.
• Cook poultry immediately after thawing, or keep it in the refrigerator until you're ready to cook it up to one day.

*Cooking*
• Cook poultry until it's thoroughly done; never leave it medium or rare. Whole chickens or turkeys should be cooked to an internal temperature of 180° and bone-in parts cooked to 170°. When juices run clear as the meat is pierced with a fork, it's a sign the chicken or turkey is done.

# Chicken and Artichoke Pizzas

**Time:** prep 5 minutes; cook 16 minutes

| | |
|---|---|
| ¼ | cup no-salt-added tomato sauce |
| 1 | teaspoon dried Italian seasoning |
| 1 | clove garlic, minced |
| 2 | (7-inch) pita bread rounds |
| ¼ | cup sliced cooked chicken breast (skinned before cooking and cooked without salt and fat) |
| ½ | cup canned quartered artichoke hearts, drained |
| ½ | cup (2 ounces) shredded 50% less-fat mozzarella cheese |
| ¼ | cup chopped onion |
| 2 | tablespoons drained sliced ripe olives |

**1.** Combine first 3 ingredients in a small bowl, stirring well. Spread tomato sauce mixture evenly over tops of pita bread rounds. Layer chicken and artichoke evenly over sauce; sprinkle evenly with cheese, onion, and olives. Place pizzas on an ungreased baking sheet.

**2.** Bake at 400° for 16 minutes or until cheese melts and pitas are golden. Yield: 2 servings.

## ✐ *t i p*

*Chicken is moister and easier to slice if you cook the breast halves first. Allow the cooked chicken to cool slightly before slicing it.*

Bean Salad on Greens (*recipe, page 112*)

97

Chinese Chicken Salad (*recipe, pages 120 and 121*)

# Sweet-and-Sour Chicken

**Time:** prep 10 minutes; cook 10 minutes

Vegetable cooking spray
2     teaspoons vegetable oil
1     medium onion, cut into wedges
½     medium-size sweet red pepper, seeded and cut into thin strips
1½   pounds skinned, boned chicken breasts, cut into thin strips
2     cups snow pea pods, stem ends and strings removed
1     cup bean sprouts
½     cup sweet-and-sour sauce
¼     teaspoon ground cumin
3     cups hot cooked fettuccine (cooked without salt or fat)

**Each Serving Provides:**

3 Protein/Milk
1 Bread
1 Fruit/Vegetable
40 Optional Calories

**Per Serving:**

280 Calories
31.6g Carbohydrate
3.6g Fat (0.7g saturated)
4.2g Fiber
31.0g Protein
66mg Cholesterol
119mg Sodium
47mg Calcium
2.7mg Iron

**1.** Coat a wok or large nonstick skillet with cooking spray. Drizzle oil around top of wok, coating sides; place over medium-high heat until hot. Add onion and red pepper, and stir-fry 2 to 3 minutes or until vegetables are tender. Add chicken, and stir-fry 3 to 4 minutes or until chicken is browned.

**2.** Add snow peas and bean sprouts to chicken mixture; stir-fry 1 to 2 minutes or until peas are crisp-tender. Stir in sweet-and-sour sauce and cumin. Bring to a boil; reduce heat to low, and simmer 4 to 5 minutes or until mixture is thoroughly heated.

**3.** Place ½ cup fettuccine on each of 6 individual serving plates; top fettuccine evenly with chicken mixture. Yield: 6 servings.

*tip*

*You don't have to have a wok to prepare stir-fry recipes. Just use a large skillet and make sure it's hot before adding the ingredients so they will cook quickly to crisp-tender.*

# Chicken with Brandy Sauce

**Time:** prep 5 minutes; cook 21 minutes

Vegetable cooking spray

1   teaspoon vegetable oil

4   (4-ounce) skinned, boned chicken breast halves

4   cups sliced fresh mushrooms

½   cup canned no-salt-added chicken broth, undiluted

3   tablespoons brandy

1   tablespoon low-sodium soy sauce

¼   teaspoon freshly ground pepper

**1.** Coat a large nonstick skillet with cooking spray, and add oil; place over medium-high heat until hot. Add chicken, and cook 6 to 8 minutes on each side or until chicken is done. Transfer chicken to a serving platter. Set aside, and keep warm.

**2.** Add mushrooms to skillet; cook 3 minutes, stirring often. Stir in chicken broth and remaining 3 ingredients. Bring to a boil; reduce heat to low, and simmer, uncovered, 6 minutes. Spoon mushroom mixture over chicken. Yield: 4 servings.

## ✎ *tip*

*If you don't have brandy, you can substitute the same amount of white wine for a savory sauce.*

# Grilled Lemon Chicken

**Time:** prep 8 minutes; marinate 2 hours; cook 10 minutes

Zest of 1 lemon
2   tablespoons fresh lemon juice
1   cup sliced green onions
1   tablespoon chopped fresh parsley
1   tablespoon chopped fresh basil or 1 teaspoon dried basil
2   cloves garlic, minced
6   (4-ounce) skinned, boned chicken breast halves
Vegetable cooking spray

**1.** Combine first 6 ingredients in a large heavy-duty, zip-top plastic bag; add chicken. Seal bag and turn to coat chicken. Marinate in refrigerator at least 2 hours, turning bag occasionally.

**2.** Remove chicken from marinade, and discard marinade.

**3.** Coat grill rack with cooking spray; place on grill over medium-hot coals (350° to 400°). Place chicken on rack, and grill, covered, 5 minutes on each side or until chicken is done. Yield: 6 servings.

**Each Serving Provides:**
3 Protein/Milk

**Per Serving:**
150 Calories
2.3g Carbohydrate
3.2g Fat (0.9g saturated)
0.4g Fiber
26.8g Protein
72mg Cholesterol
66mg Sodium
29mg Calcium
1.2mg Iron

*tip*

*A handy device called a zester helps you scrape delicate shards of rind from citrus fruit without cutting into the bitter white membrane beneath the rind.*

# Chicken with Herbs and Citrus

**Time:** prep 5 minutes; cook 10 minutes

**Each Serving Provides:**

3 Protein/Milk

**Per Serving:**

151 Calories

2.8g Carbohydrate

3.3g Fat (0.9g saturated)

0.3g Fiber

26.7g Protein

72mg Cholesterol

210mg Sodium

23mg Calcium

1.2mg Iron

| | |
|---|---|
| 4 | (4-ounce) skinned, boned chicken breast halves |
| 1 | teaspoon paprika |
| ¼ | teaspoon freshly ground pepper |
| 2 | tablespoons chopped fresh basil |
| 2 | tablespoons chopped fresh thyme |
| 3 | tablespoons fresh lemon juice |
| 3 | tablespoons fresh lime juice |
| ¼ | teaspoon salt |

Vegetable cooking spray

**1.** Sprinkle chicken evenly with paprika and pepper. Combine basil and next 4 ingredients in a small bowl; stir well.

**2.** Coat grill rack with cooking spray; place on grill over medium-hot coals (350° to 400°). Place chicken on rack; brush with half of herb mixture. Grill, covered, 5 minutes; turn chicken and brush with remaining herb mixture. Cover and grill 5 additional minutes or until chicken is done. Yield: 4 servings.

## ✎ *tip*

*Try this to determine grill temperature: If you can hold your hand, palm-side down, at grill rack level for only 3 seconds before having to pull your hand away, the coals are medium-hot.*

# Grilled Dijon Chicken *(photo, page 80)*

**Time:** prep 5 minutes; cook 10 minutes

| 1 | tablespoon brown sugar |
|---|---|
| 2 | tablespoons Dijon mustard |
| 1 | tablespoon honey |
| 1 | teaspoon peeled, minced gingerroot |

Vegetable cooking spray

| 4 | (4-ounce) skinned, boned chicken breast halves |
|---|---|

Fresh parsley sprigs (optional)

**1.** Combine first 4 ingredients in a small bowl; stir well.

**2.** Coat grill rack with cooking spray; place on grill over medium-hot coals. Place chicken on rack, and brush half of mustard mixture over chicken. Grill, covered, 5 minutes; turn chicken, and brush with remaining mustard mixture. Cover and grill 5 additional minutes or until chicken is done. Transfer chicken to a serving platter, and garnish with parsley, if desired. Yield: 4 servings.

*Note:* To bake, place chicken in an 11- x 7- x 1½-inch baking dish coated with cooking spray. Brush mustard mixture over chicken. Cover and bake at 375° for 15 to 20 minutes or until chicken is done. Uncover and broil chicken 4 inches from heat (with electric oven door partially opened) 1 to 2 minutes or until golden.

**Each Serving Provides:**

3 Protein/Milk

**Per Serving:**

176 Calories

7.1g Carbohydrate

3.7g Fat (0.9g saturated)

0.0g Fiber

26.4g Protein

72mg Cholesterol

287mg Sodium

15mg Calcium

0.9mg Iron

*tip*

*Measure dry ingredients before wet ones so you can use the same measuring spoon or cup without washing it.*

# Baked Couscous Chicken

**Time:** prep 5 minutes; cook 37 minutes

**Each Serving Provides:**

3 Protein/Milk

2 Bread

1 Fruit/Vegetable

1 Fat

**Per Serving:**

369 Calories

46.4g Carbohydrate

4.9g Fat (0.7g saturated)

3.5g Fiber

35.1g Protein

66mg Cholesterol

98mg Sodium

41mg Calcium

3.2mg Iron

Vegetable cooking spray

2    teaspoons olive oil

4    (4-ounce) skinned, boned chicken breast halves

4    cloves garlic, crushed

1    cup sliced green onions

2    cups sliced mushrooms

1    medium tomato, chopped

½    cup canned low-sodium chicken broth, undiluted

½    teaspoon freshly ground pepper

1    sprig fresh thyme

4    cups hot cooked couscous (cooked without salt or fat)

**1.** Coat a 2-quart casserole dish or ovenproof Dutch oven with cooking spray, and add oil; place over medium-high heat until hot. Add chicken, and cook 3 to 4 minutes on each side or until chicken is lightly browned. Add garlic, and cook 1 to 2 additional minutes, stirring often.

**2.** Stir in green onions and next 5 ingredients. Cover and bake at 350° for 30 to 35 minutes or until chicken is tender.

**3.** Place 1 cup of couscous on each of 4 individual serving plates; spoon chicken mixture evenly over couscous. Yield: 4 servings.

## ✑ *t i p*

*Crush garlic on a cutting board using the blade of a large knife. Place the blade flat on top of a garlic clove; press until the garlic is crushed.*

# Chicken with Orzo and Herbs

**Time:** prep 5 minutes; cook 35 minutes

| | |
|---|---|
| 4 | (5-ounce) skinned bone-in chicken pieces |

Vegetable cooking spray

| | |
|---|---|
| 6 | ounces orzo (rice-shaped pasta), uncooked |
| 1½ | cups chopped onion |
| 1½ | cups chopped plum tomatoes |
| 1½ | cups canned low-sodium chicken broth, undiluted |
| ¾ | cup water |
| ¼ | cup minced fresh parsley |
| 3 | cloves garlic, minced |
| 1 | teaspoon fresh thyme |
| ½ | teaspoon dried oregano |
| ¼ | teaspoon freshly ground pepper |
| ⅓ | cup freshly grated Parmesan cheese |

**Each Serving Provides:**

3 Protein/Milk

2 Bread

1 Fruit/Vegetable

**Per Serving:**

370 Calories

42.8g Carbohydrate

5.2g Fat (1.8g saturated)

3.4g Fiber

36.9g Protein

71mg Cholesterol

239mg Sodium

141mg Calcium

3.8mg Iron

**1.** Arrange chicken in a 13- x 9- x 2-inch baking dish coated with cooking spray. Combine orzo and next 9 ingredients in a large bowl; pour over chicken.

**2.** Bake, covered, at 350° for 30 minutes; sprinkle cheese evenly over top of casserole. Uncover, and bake 5 to 10 additional minutes or until orzo is tender and chicken is done. Yield: 4 servings.

*tip*

*Save time by preheating the oven anytime you prepare a recipe that bakes or roasts.*

# Chicken Paprika

**Time:** prep 5 minutes; cook 40 minutes

Vegetable cooking spray

1 tablespoon margarine

1 cup chopped onion

8 (3-ounce) skinned chicken drumsticks

1 (15-ounce) can no-salt-added crushed tomatoes, undrained

¾ cup water

1 tablespoon paprika

1 teaspoon chicken-flavored bouillon granules

⅛ teaspoon freshly ground pepper

4 cups hot cooked rice (cooked without salt or fat)

⅓ cup nonfat sour cream

**1.** Coat a large nonstick skillet with cooking spray, and add margarine; place over medium-high heat until margarine melts. Add onion, and cook 5 minutes or until tender, stirring often. Add chicken to skillet, and cook, until chicken is browned, turning often.

**2.** Add tomato and next 4 ingredients; bring to a boil. Reduce heat to low, and simmer, covered, 30 to 40 minutes or until chicken is tender. Remove from heat.

**3.** Arrange 1 cup rice on each of 4 individual serving plates. Place two drumsticks on each plate.

**4.** Stir sour cream into tomato mixture remaining in skillet. Spoon tomato mixture evenly over chicken and rice. Yield: 4 servings.

## ✿ *t i p*

*For quick cooked rice, use the boil-in-bag kind; it cooks in half the time of regular rice. And there is no cleanup.*

*salads*

# Radicchio-Pear Salad

**Time:** prep 5 minutes

**Each Serving Provides:**

1 Fruit/Vegetable

**Per Serving:**

64 Calories

13.8g Carbohydrate

1.1g Fat (0.5g saturated)

2.2g Fiber

1.2g Protein

2mg Cholesterol

43mg Sodium

30mg Calcium

0.2mg Iron

| 4 | small ripe pears, cored and cut into eighths |
| 2 | tablespoons fresh lemon juice |
| 24 | small radicchio leaves |
| ½ | cup watercress leaves |
| 3 | tablespoons (¾ ounce) Gorgonzola cheese, crumbled |

**1.** Dip pear slices in lemon juice to prevent browning.

**2.** Arrange radicchio, pear slices, and watercress leaves evenly on 8 salad plates. Top salads evenly with cheese. Serve immediately, or cover and chill at least 1 hour. Yield: 8 servings.

*⚘ t i p*

*To ripen pears quickly, place them in a paper bag, fold down the top, and allow the bag to stand at room temperature for several hours or overnight.*

# Apple Coleslaw

**Time:** prep 10 minutes; chill 2 hours

¾  cup plain nonfat yogurt
½  cup reduced-calorie mayonnaise
2  tablespoons Dijon mustard
2  tablespoons cider vinegar
½  teaspoon salt
¼  teaspoon freshly ground pepper
5  cups shredded cabbage
5  cups shredded red cabbage
2  cups shredded carrot
½  cup chopped green onions
1  Granny Smith apple, cored and chopped

**1.** Combine first 6 ingredients in a bowl, stirring well. Set aside.

**2.** Combine cabbages and remaining 3 ingredients in a large bowl; add yogurt mixture, and toss well to mix. Cover and chill at least 2 hours. Yield: 12 servings.

**Each Serving Provides:**

1 Fruit/Vegetable

1 Fat

**Per Serving:**

70 Calories

9.4g Carbohydrate

3.0g Fat (0.7g saturated)

2.6g Fiber

2.0g Protein

4mg Cholesterol

278mg Sodium

68mg Calcium

0.6mg Iron

*✿ t i p*

*You cut preparation time for this recipe in half when you use packages of shredded cabbage and carrot.*

# Caesar Salad

**Time:** prep 5 minutes; cook 10 minutes

1½  cups cubed French bread (about 4 slices)
Olive oil-flavored vegetable cooking spray
1     clove garlic, halved
7     cups torn romaine lettuce
¼    cup freshly grated Parmesan cheese
½    cup fat-free Caesar salad dressing

**1.** Coat bread cubes with cooking spray; arrange in a single layer on a baking sheet. Bake at 350° for 10 minutes or until lightly browned, and set aside.

**2.** Rub inside of a large salad bowl with cut sides of garlic; discard garlic. Combine lettuce, Parmesan cheese, and bread cubes in salad bowl. Pour Caesar dressing over salad, and toss well. Serve immediately. Yield: 4 servings.

### ✤ t i p

*Cutting bread into cubes for croutons is faster when you use a pizza cutter. Freeze the bread cubes until you need them.*

# Salad Greens with Onion Dressing

**Time:** prep 5 minutes; cook 6 minutes

2   cups torn radicchio
2   cups torn iceberg lettuce
2   cups torn curly endive
3   tablespoons chopped fresh parsley
Vegetable cooking spray
1   teaspoon olive oil
1   medium onion, sliced and separated into rings
1   tablespoon plus 1 teaspoon red wine vinegar
1   clove garlic, minced
½   teaspoon sugar

**1.** Combine first 4 ingredients in a large bowl; arrange mixture on a large serving platter, and set aside.

**2.** Coat a small nonstick skillet with cooking spray, and add oil; place over medium-high heat until hot. Add onion, and cook 5 to 7 minutes until tender, stirring often. Add vinegar, garlic, and sugar to skillet; cook, stirring constantly, 1 minute. Spoon onion mixture over salad greens, and serve immediately. Yield: 4 servings.

**Each Serving Provides:**
2 Fruit/Vegetable

**Per Serving:**
56 Calories
9.1g Carbohydrate
1.7g Fat (0.2g saturated)
1.1g Fiber
2.3g Protein
0mg Cholesterol
29mg Sodium
44mg Calcium
0.5mg Iron

*tip*

*After you slice or chop onions, rub the cutting board with fresh parsley to remove the onion odor.*

# Bean Salad on Greens *(photo, page 97)*

**Time:** prep 5 minutes; chill 30 minutes

**Each Serving Provides:**
1 Protein/Milk
1 Fruit/Vegetable

**Per Serving:**
88 Calories
14.9g Carbohydrate
1.2g Fat (0.2g saturated)
3.2g Fiber
5.2g Protein
0mg Cholesterol
275mg Sodium
28mg Calcium
1.6mg Iron

2   (15-ounce) cans black beans, drained
1   (15-ounce) can cannellini beans, drained
2   small sweet red peppers, seeded and chopped
1   cup chopped green onions
¼   cup chopped fresh cilantro
2   tablespoons fresh lime juice
2   teaspoons olive oil
1   clove garlic, minced
½   teaspoon salt
6   cups torn lettuce leaves

**1.** Combine first 5 ingredients in a large bowl, and toss to mix. Combine lime juice and next 3 ingredients in a small bowl, stirring well with a wire whisk. Pour lime juice mixture over bean mixture, tossing well. Cover and chill at least 30 minutes.

**2.** To serve, arrange ½ cup lettuce on each of 12 salad plates, and top each serving with ½ cup bean mixture. Yield: 12 servings.

*✍ t i p*

*Use a salad spinner to spin-dry freshly washed lettuce leaves; it's quick, and it makes the lettuce leaves crisper.*

# Tomato and Onion Salad

**Time:** prep 5 minutes; chill 30 minutes

| | |
|---|---|
| 6 | medium tomatoes, sliced |
| 2 | medium onions, thinly sliced |
| ¼ | cup sliced ripe olives |
| 3 | tablespoons dry white wine |
| 2 | teaspoons vegetable oil |
| 1 | teaspoon dried oregano |
| ⅛ | teaspoon freshly ground pepper |

**1.** Arrange tomato and onion slices on a serving platter; sprinkle with olives, and set aside.

**2.** Combine wine and remaining 3 ingredients in a jar; cover tightly, and shake vigorously to blend. Pour wine mixture over tomato and onion; cover and chill at least 30 minutes. Yield: 6 servings.

**Each Serving Provides:**

1 Fruit/Vegetable

1 Fat

**Per Serving:**

80 Calories

11.7g Carbohydrate

3.4g Fat (0.6g saturated)

3.1g Fiber

1.9g Protein

0mg Cholesterol

119mg Sodium

32mg Calcium

1.3mg Iron

*tip*

*If you prefer peeled tomatoes, dip them into boiling water for 15 to 30 seconds, and the skins will slip off easily.*

# Green Beans and Rotelle Salad

Time: prep 10 minutes; cook 8 minutes

**Each Serving Provides:**
1 Bread
2 Fruit/Vegetable
1 Fat

**Per Serving:**
132 Calories
23.3g Carbohydrate
2.8g Fat (0.4g saturated)
2.4g Fiber
4.6g Protein
0mg Cholesterol
13mg Sodium
48mg Calcium
2.1mg Iron

| | |
|---|---|
| 1 | cup water |
| 2 | cups fresh green beans, trimmed and cut into 2-inch pieces |
| 2 | cups cooked rotelle (corkscrew pasta), cooked without salt or fat |
| 1 | cup chopped green onions |
| 1 | (2-ounce) jar diced pimiento, drained |
| 1 | tablespoon plus 1½ teaspoons white wine vinegar |
| 1 | tablespoon plus 1½ teaspoons fresh lemon juice |
| 2 | teaspoons olive oil |
| ¼ | teaspoon dried tarragon |
| 4 | red leaf lettuce leaves |

**1.** Bring water to a boil in a medium saucepan; add beans, and cook, uncovered, 8 to 10 minutes or just until crisp-tender. Drain. Rinse under cold water, and drain well.

**2.** Combine beans, pasta, green onions, and pimiento in a large bowl; set aside.

**3.** Combine vinegar and next 3 ingredients in a jar; cover tightly, and shake vigorously to blend. Pour vinegar mixture over pasta mixture, and toss well. Spoon mixture evenly onto 4 salad plates lined with red leaf lettuce. Yield: 4 servings.

*✎ t i p*

*You'll need to cook 4 ounces of rotelle to get 2 cups of cooked pasta.*

Fruited Turkey Tabbouleh *(recipe, page 124)*; Basil Yogurt Cheese *(recipe, page 129)*

115

Thai Shrimp Salad *(recipe, page 126)*

Peppers Braised with Herbs (*recipe, page 141*)

Crispy Potato Pancake (*recipe, page 144*)

# Vegetable-Noodle Salad

**Time:** prep 10 minutes; chill 1 hour

| | |
|---|---|
| 3 | ounces spaghetti, uncooked |
| 1 | (8-ounce) can sliced water chestnuts, drained |
| 1 | (7¾-ounce) can garbanzo beans, drained |
| ⅓ | cup chopped green pepper |
| ⅓ | cup chopped sweet red pepper |
| 3 | tablespoons reduced-calorie mayonnaise |
| 2 | tablespoons low-sodium soy sauce |
| ¼ | teaspoon hot sauce |
| ⅛ | teaspoon salt |
| ⅛ | teaspoon garlic powder |

**Each Serving Provides:**

1 Protein/Milk

1 Bread

1 Fruit/Vegetable

**Per Serving:**

177 Calories

29.7g Carbohydrate

3.8g Fat (0.8g saturated)

3.7g Fiber

6.0g Protein

4mg Cholesterol

443mg Sodium

7mg Calcium

1.4mg Iron

**1.** Cook spaghetti according to package directions, omitting salt and fat; drain. Rinse under cold water; drain again.

**2.** Combine spaghetti, water chestnuts, and next 3 ingredients in a large bowl; toss gently. Combine mayonnaise and remaining 4 ingredients; stir well. Add mayonnaise mixture to pasta mixture; toss well. Cover and chill at least 1 hour. Yield: 4 servings.

# Chinese Chicken Salad (photo, page 98)

**Time:** prep 15 minutes; marinate 1 hour; cook 16 minutes

**Each Serving Provides:**

2 Protein/Milk
1 Bread
2 Fruit/Vegetable
70 Optional Calories

**Per Serving:**

287 Calories
35.8g Carbohydrate
3.4g Fat (0.5g saturated)
4.4g Fiber
28.0g Protein
55mg Cholesterol
217mg Sodium
95mg Calcium
3.6mg Iron

| | |
|---|---|
| 1 | cup orange juice |
| 2 | tablespoons low-sodium soy sauce |
| 2 | tablespoons honey |
| 1¼ | pounds skinned, boned chicken breast, cut into thin strips |
| 4½ | ounces angel hair pasta, uncooked |
| | Vegetable cooking spray |
| ½ | cup chopped fresh cilantro |
| 3 | tablespoons rice wine vinegar |
| 1½ | cups water |
| 3 | cups snow pea pods, trimmed |
| 6 | cups thinly sliced napa cabbage |
| 1 | cup sliced radishes |
| ¼ | cup chopped green onions |
| 2 | tablespoons chopped almonds, toasted |

**⚜ t i p**

*To toast almonds, spread 2 tablespoons of chopped nuts in a pieplate, and microwave at HIGH for 1 minute or until toasted. Stir once during the cooking time.*

**1.** Combine orange juice, soy sauce, and honey in a large heavy-duty, zip-top plastic bag; add chicken. Seal bag, and turn bag to coat chicken. Marinate in refrigerator 1 hour.

**2.** Prepare pasta according to package directions, omitting salt and fat. Drain and rinse under cold water; drain again. Place in a large bowl; cover and set aside.

**3.** Remove chicken from marinade, reserving marinade. Coat a wok or large nonstick skillet with cooking spray; place over medium-high heat until hot. Add chicken; stir-fry 3 to 4 minutes or until chicken is lightly browned. Add marinade to skillet, and bring to a boil. Reduce heat to low; cover and simmer 10 minutes or until chicken is done. Stir in cilantro and vinegar.

**4.** Pour chicken mixture over pasta, stirring well; set aside.

**5.** Bring 1½ cups water to a boil in a medium saucepan; add snow peas. Cover and cook 3 to 5 minutes or until crisp-tender; drain and place in a large bowl. Cool slightly. Add cabbage, radishes, and green onions to snow peas, tossing well. Arrange mixture evenly on 6 individual serving plates. Spoon pasta mixture evenly over cabbage mixture; sprinkle with almonds. Yield: 6 servings.

## How To Make a Tossed Salad (Without Iceberg Lettuce)

You've made tossed salad with iceberg lettuce for years. Now you can choose from a wide variety of leafy greens to change the flavor, texture, and color of any salad. For a sweet and succulent flavor, try Boston or butterhead lettuce. Toss in some watercress or arugula for a peppery taste.

To add a bitter bite to salad, mix in curly endive, escarole, romaine lettuce, radicchio, or dandelion, turnip, or collard greens. Purple-leaved radicchio adds crisp texture, too. Sometimes you can find bags of mixed bitter greens in the produce section; it's a great way to sample them all.

# Fruity Chicken Salad

**Time:** prep 10 minutes

**Each Serving Provides:**

2 Protein/Milk
3 Fruit/Vegetable
50 Optional Calories

**Per Serving:**

203 Calories
17.8g Carbohydrate
7.2g Fat (3.5g saturated)
2.3g Fiber
17.4g Protein
47mg Cholesterol
249mg Sodium
121mg Calcium
1.0mg Iron

| | |
|---|---|
| 1 | cup chopped cooked chicken breast (skinned before cooking and cooked without salt or fat) |
| 1 | large pear, cored and thinly sliced |
| 8 | pitted dates, cut into thin strips |
| ⅔ | cup sliced celery (about 2 stalks) |
| ⅓ | cup (2.6 ounces) diced Camembert cheese |
| 2 | tablespoons fat-free honey mustard salad dressing |
| 2 | teaspoons orange zest |
| 2 | tablespoons fresh orange juice |
| 2 | tablespoons plain nonfat yogurt |
| 4 | cups torn lettuce leaves |
| 2 | teaspoons unsalted sunflower seeds |

**1.** Combine first 5 ingredients in a large bowl. Combine salad dressing and next 3 ingredients in a bowl; add to chicken mixture, and toss gently. Spoon mixture onto a large lettuce-lined serving platter. Sprinkle with sunflower seeds. Yield: 4 servings.

## ✍ *tip*

*Coat kitchen shears with cooking spray, and use them to cut the dates into strips. Cooking spray keeps the dates from sticking to the shears.*

# BLT Salad

**Time:** prep 10 minutes; chill 1 hour

| 8 | ounces elbow macaroni, uncooked |
| ¼ | cup plus 2 tablespoons reduced-calorie mayonnaise |
| ¼ | cup plus 2 tablespoons plain nonfat yogurt |
| ¼ | cup plus 2 tablespoons chili sauce |
| 2 | tablespoons lemon juice |
| 1 | teaspoon sugar |
| ¼ | teaspoon salt |
| 1 | large tomato, seeded and chopped |
| ¼ | cup chopped green onions |
| 4 | cups thinly sliced lettuce |
| 6 | slices turkey bacon, chopped, cooked, and drained |

**1.** Cook macaroni according to package directions, omitting salt and fat; drain. Rinse under cold water; drain again.

**2.** Combine macaroni, mayonnaise, and next 8 ingredients in a large bowl; cover and chill at least 1 hour. Sprinkle with bacon just before serving. Yield: 6 servings.

**Each Serving Provides:**

2 Bread
1 Fruit/Vegetable
2 Fat

**Per Serving:**

249 Calories
37.5g Carbohydrate
6.8g Fat (1.7g saturated)
1.7g Fiber
8.8g Protein
15mg Cholesterol
656mg Sodium
50mg Calcium
1.9mg Iron

*tip*

*To get a jump on this recipe, cook the macaroni a day in advance and chill it.*

# Fruited Turkey Tabbouleh *(photo, page 115)*

**Time:** prep 10 minutes; cook 30 minutes; chill 1 hour

**Each Serving Provides:**

2 Protein/Milk
1 Bread
2 Fruit/Vegetable
1 Fat

**Per Serving:**

324 Calories
45.7g Carbohydrate
8.0g Fat (1.5g saturated)
8.4g Fiber
22.9g Protein
38mg Cholesterol
663mg Sodium
50mg Calcium
3.6mg Iron

| | |
|---|---|
| 1 | cup bulgur (cracked wheat), uncooked |
| 2 | cups boiling water |
| 1 | red apple, cored and chopped |
| ¼ | cup fresh lemon juice |
| 1½ | cups chopped smoked turkey |
| 1 | cup red grape halves |
| ¼ | cup raisins |
| ¼ | cup chopped fresh parsley |
| ¼ | cup chopped fresh mint |
| 3 | tablespoons chopped walnuts |
| 1 | tablespoon oil-free Italian salad dressing |
| ¼ | teaspoon salt |
| 1 | cucumber, peeled, seeded, and chopped |
| 1 | head radicchio |

*✎ t i p*

*Buy about ¾ pound of smoked turkey from the deli to get 1½ cups of chopped smoked turkey.*

**1.** Combine bulgur and water in a bowl; let stand 30 minutes. Drain and squeeze in several layers of damp cheesecloth or dry paper towels. Place bulgur in a large bowl.

**2.** Combine apple and lemon juice in a large bowl, stirring to coat apple. Add bulgur, turkey, and next 8 ingredients. Cover and chill at least 1 hour. Arrange radicchio on 4 salad plates; spoon tabbouleh evenly over radicchio. Yield: 4 servings.

# Crunchy Spinach Salad with Ham

**Time:** prep 8 minutes; cook 9 minutes

Vegetable cooking spray
1     clove garlic, minced
¼    cup cider vinegar
¼    cup orange juice
¼    cup honey
1     teaspoon olive oil
1½   cups sliced fresh mushrooms
1     cup diced cooked lean ham
4     cups torn fresh spinach leaves
1½   cups bean sprouts
4     (1-ounce) slices multi-grain bread, cubed and toasted
¼    cup freshly grated Parmesan cheese
¼    cup chopped fresh basil
¼    cup chopped fresh parsley

**Each Serving Provides:**

2 Protein/Milk
1 Bread
2 Fruit/Vegetable
40 Optional Calories

**Per Serving:**

232 Calories
33.3g Carbohydrate
6.5g Fat (3.6g saturated)
6.0g Fiber
15.5g Protein
28mg Cholesterol
806mg Sodium
178mg Calcium
3.7mg Iron

**1.** Coat a large nonstick skillet with cooking spray; place over medium-high heat until hot. Add garlic, and cook, stirring constantly, 1 minute. Stir in vinegar, orange juice, and honey; bring to a boil, stirring constantly. Remove mixture from skillet; cool slightly.

**2.** Wipe skillet with a paper towel; add oil, and place over medium-high heat until hot. Add mushrooms and ham, and cook 5 minutes or until mushrooms are tender, stirring often; set aside.

**3.** Combine spinach and bean sprouts in a large serving bowl; add mushroom mixture, and toss to combine.

**4.** Drizzle reserved orange juice mixture over salad; toss to coat. Add bread cubes, cheese, basil, and parsley; toss well. Yield: 4 servings.

*tip*

*Buy packages of prewashed fresh spinach leaves to save time.*

# Thai Shrimp Salad *(photo, page 116)*

**Time:** prep 20 minutes; cook 3 minutes; chill 2 hours

| | |
|---|---|
| 4 | cups water |
| 1¼ | pounds unpeeled medium-size fresh shrimp |
| 2 | cucumbers, peeled, quartered lengthwise, seeded, and sliced |
| ⅓ | cup fresh lime juice |
| ¼ | teaspoon salt |
| ½ | cup chopped green onions |
| 1 | sweet red pepper, seeded and cut into thin strips |
| ¼ | cup reduced-fat coconut milk |
| ¼ | cup plain nonfat yogurt |
| ¼ | teaspoon dried crushed red pepper |
| ¼ | cup chopped fresh cilantro |
| 3 | cups baby salad greens |
| 3 | tablespoons roasted peanuts |

*✦ t i p*

*Most of the prep time for this recipe is spent peeling the shrimp. Buy the shrimp already cooked and peeled to save time.*

**1.** Bring water to a boil; add shrimp, and cook 3 to 5 minutes or until shrimp turn pink. Drain well; rinse with cold water. Chill. Peel and devein shrimp.

**2.** Place sliced cucumber on paper towels; allow to drain 10 minutes.

**3.** Combine shrimp, lime juice, and salt in a large bowl; stir in cucumber, green onions, and sweet red pepper.

**4.** Combine coconut milk, yogurt, and crushed red pepper; pour over shrimp mixture, and stir well. Stir in cilantro. Cover and chill at least 1 hour.

**5.** Arrange salad greens on 4 salad plates; spoon shrimp mixture evenly over greens. Sprinkle evenly with peanuts. Yield: 4 servings.

*sides*

# Mango-Kiwi Salsa *(photo, page 155)*

**Time:** prep 8 minutes; chill 2 hours

3   small mangoes, peeled and chopped
3   kiwifruit, peeled and chopped
1   medium-size sweet red pepper, diced
¼   cup chopped onion
2   tablespoons fresh lemon juice
¼   teaspoon salt
⅛   teaspoon ground red pepper

**1.** Combine all ingredients in a large bowl; cover and chill at least 2 hours. Serve salsa with pork, chicken, or fish. Yield: 4 cups (¼ cup salsa per serving).

*✿ t i p*

*Ripe mangoes are as soft as bananas. To ripen them quickly, place them in a paper bag at room temperature for a day.*

# Basil Yogurt Cheese *(photo, page 115)*

**Time:** prep 10 minutes

1     (16-ounce) carton plain nonfat yogurt
1     tablespoon chopped fresh basil
¼     teaspoon garlic powder
¼     teaspoon salt
1     sprig fresh basil (optional)

**1.** Spoon yogurt onto several layers of heavy-duty paper towels; spread to ½-inch thickness. Cover with additional paper towels; let stand 5 minutes. Scrape yogurt into a bowl using a rubber spatula. Add next 3 ingredients, and stir well. Garnish with fresh basil sprig, if desired. Serve with fresh vegetables or as a topping for baked potatoes. Yield: 1 cup (1 tablespoon per serving).

*Note:* Be sure to use yogurt that does not have added gelatin. Less expensive brands of yogurt often use gelatin as a thickener.

**Each Serving Provides:**
Free

**Per Serving:**
16 Calories
2.2g Carbohydrate
0.0g Fat (0.0g saturated)
0.0g Fiber
1.6g Protein
1mg Cholesterol
58mg Sodium
57mg Calcium
0.0mg Iron

## *tip*

*You can substitute nonfat sour cream for nonfat yogurt. For more intense basil and garlic flavors, chill the mixture overnight before serving.*

# Maple-Ginger Beans

**Time:** prep 5 minutes; cook 20 minutes

Vegetable cooking spray

| | |
|---|---|
| 1 | teaspoon reduced-calorie margarine |
| ½ | cup chopped onion |
| 2 | cloves garlic, minced |
| 1 | (15-ounce) can cannellini beans, drained |
| ¼ | cup reduced-calorie maple-flavored syrup |
| ¼ | cup water |
| 2 | tablespoons hot salsa |
| 1 | teaspoon dry mustard |
| 1 | teaspoon hot sauce |
| ¼ | teaspoon ground ginger |
| ¼ | teaspoon ground cloves |

**1.** Coat a medium saucepan with cooking spray, and add margarine; place over medium-high heat until margarine melts. Add onion and garlic, and cook 4 to 5 minutes or until onion is tender, stirring often.

**2.** Stir in beans and remaining ingredients; bring to a boil. Reduce heat to low; cover, and simmer 15 to 20 minutes, stirring often. Yield: 4 servings.

## tip

*After mincing garlic, rub salt or the cut edge of a lemon over the cutting board surface to remove the garlic odor.*

# Red Beans with Herbs

**Time:** prep 8 minutes; cook 25 minutes

Vegetable cooking spray
1   teaspoon vegetable oil
1   cup chopped onion
½   cup chopped celery
½   cup chopped green pepper
3   cloves garlic, minced
1   (19-ounce) can kidney beans, drained
1   cup canned low-sodium chicken broth, undiluted
½   teaspoon dried thyme
1   bay leaf
2   tablespoons chopped fresh parsley

**1.** Coat a medium nonstick skillet with cooking spray, and add oil; place over medium-high heat until hot. Add onion, celery, and pepper, and cook 8 minutes or until vegetables are tender, stirring often. Add garlic; cook 2 additional minutes. Stir in beans and next 3 ingredients; reduce heat to low, and simmer, uncovered, 15 minutes. Stir mixture occasionally.

**2.** Remove and discard bay leaf. Transfer one-fourth of bean mixture to a small bowl, using a slotted spoon; mash beans with a fork. Return mashed beans to broth mixture, stirring well. Stir in parsley. Yield: 4 servings.

**Each Serving Provides:**

1 Protein/Milk
1 Fruit/Vegetable
50 Optional Calories

**Per Serving:**

164 Calories
27.8g Carbohydrate
2.3g Fat (0.3g saturated)
4.8g Fiber
9.6g Protein
0mg Cholesterol
38mg Sodium
51mg Calcium
3.7mg Iron

*tip*

*Keep dried herbs fresh by storing them in jars in the freezer.*

# Green Beans with Onion and Garlic

**Time:** prep 5 minutes; cook 18 minutes

2     cups fresh green beans
1     cup water
Vegetable cooking spray
2     teaspoons margarine
1     medium onion, thinly sliced
2     cloves garlic, minced

**1.** Wash beans, and remove strings. Place in a large saucepan; add water, and bring to a boil. Cover, reduce heat, and simmer 12 to 15 minutes or until beans are tender. Drain.

**2.** Coat a large skillet with cooking spray, and add margarine; place over medium-high heat until margarine melts. Add onion and garlic, and cook 5 to 7 minutes or until onion is tender, stirring often. Add green beans to skillet, and cook 1 minute or until beans are thoroughly heated, stirring often. Yield: 4 servings.

*✎ tip*

*If you don't have fresh green beans on hand, substitute frozen beans in this recipe.*

# Cauliflower with Cheese Sauce

**Time:** prep 5 minutes; cook 26 minutes

3  cups cauliflower flowerets
1  cup water
Vegetable cooking spray
1  tablespoon reduced-calorie margarine
2  tablespoons all-purpose flour
2  cups skim milk
¾  cup (3 ounces) shredded reduced-fat sharp Cheddar cheese,
     divided
⅛  teaspoon paprika
3  tablespoons chopped fresh parsley

**Each Serving Provides:**
1 Protein/Milk
1 Fruit/Vegetable

**Per Serving:**
105 Calories
9.0g Carbohydrate
4.3g Fat (2.0g saturated)
1.4g Fiber
8.3g Protein
11mg Cholesterol
182mg Sodium
226mg Calcium
0.5mg Iron

**1.** Place cauliflower in a medium saucepan; add water, and bring to a boil. Cover, reduce heat, and simmer 8 to 10 minutes or until crisp-tender; drain. Place cauliflower in a 1-quart casserole coated with cooking spray; set aside.

**2.** Melt margarine in a small, heavy saucepan over medium heat; add flour. Cook, stirring constantly with a wire whisk, 1 minute. Gradually add milk, stirring constantly. Cook, stirring constantly, 10 additional minutes or until thickened and bubbly. Remove from heat; add ½ cup cheese, stirring until cheese melts.

**3.** Pour cheese mixture over cauliflower, stirring to mix well. Sprinkle remaining ¼ cup cheese and paprika over casserole. Bake, uncovered, at 350° for 15 to 20 minutes or until top is golden. Sprinkle with parsley. Yield: 6 servings.

*tip*

*To save time, use packages of cauliflower flowerets rather than separating your own flowerets.*

# Corn and Onion Pancakes

**Time:** prep 20 minutes; chill 30 minutes; cook 24 minutes

| | |
|---|---|
| 1 | tablespoon plus 1 teaspoon reduced-calorie margarine, softened |
| ¼ | teaspoon chili powder |
| ¾ | cup all-purpose flour |
| 2 | teaspoons baking powder |
| ¼ | teaspoon salt |
| ½ | cup skim milk |
| ¼ | cup egg substitute |
| ½ | cup cooked corn kernels |
| ¼ | cup sliced green onion tops |

Vegetable cooking spray

**1.** Combine margarine and chili powder in a small bowl; cover and chill at least 30 minutes.

**2.** Combine flour, baking powder, and salt in a small bowl; set aside. Combine milk and egg substitute; add to dry ingredients, stirring just until combined. Fold in corn and onion tops; let stand 15 minutes or until mixture is slightly thickened.

**3.** For each pancake, spoon ¼ cup batter onto a hot griddle or skillet coated with cooking spray. Cook until tops are covered with bubbles and edges look cooked; turn and cook other side. Serve pancakes with chili spread. Yield: 4 servings (2 pancakes and 1 teaspoon chili spread per serving).

## tip

*To get ½ cup cooked corn, use thawed frozen corn kernels or half of an 8¾-ounce can of whole kernel corn.*

Red Pepper-Tomato Soup *(recipe, page 152)*; Grilled Cheese *(recipe, page 157)*

*135*

136      Hearty Vegetable-Beef Soup *(recipe, page 153)*

Veggie Burgers *(recipe, page 159)*

137

Lamb Meatball Pitas *(recipe, pages 160 and 161)*

# Lemon-Herbed Mushrooms

**Time:** prep 5 minutes; cook 15 minutes

2½  (8-ounce) packages small fresh mushrooms
2  teaspoons salt-free herb-and-spice blend
¼  teaspoon grated lemon rind
⅛  teaspoon salt

**1.** Place mushrooms in a 13- x 9- x 2-inch baking dish; sprinkle with herb-and-spice blend, lemon rind, and salt. Cover and bake at 350° for 15 minutes. Yield: 6 servings.

**Each Serving Provides:**
1 Fruit/Vegetable

**Per Serving:**
22 Calories
4.1g Carbohydrate
0.3g Fat (0.0g saturated)
0.9g Fiber
1.6g Protein
0mg Cholesterol
53mg Sodium
4mg Calcium
0.9mg Iron

## ✿ t i p

*Don't wash the dirt off the mushrooms until you are ready to use them; they'll keep longer. Then use a mushroom brush or a damp paper towel to clean them just before cooking.*

# Mushroom Kabobs *(photo, page 2)*

**Time:** prep 10 minutes; cook 4 minutes

*✎ t i p*

*When you're pressed for time, use bottled fat-free Italian dressing instead of mixing the soy sauce marinade.*

| | |
|---|---|
| ¼ | cup low-sodium soy sauce |
| 1 | teaspoon Italian seasoning |
| ½ | teaspoon peeled, minced gingerroot |
| 1 | clove garlic, minced |
| 24 | whole medium-size fresh mushrooms |
| 1 | medium onion, cut into eighths |
| 8 | cherry tomatoes |
| ½ | medium-size green pepper, seeded and cut into 1-inch pieces |
| ½ | medium-size sweet red pepper, seeded and cut into 1-inch pieces |
| ½ | medium-size sweet yellow pepper, seeded and cut into 1-inch pieces |

Vegetable cooking spray

| | |
|---|---|
| 2 | cups hot cooked long-grain rice (cooked without salt or fat) |
| 1 | tablespoon chopped fresh oregano |
| 4 | sprigs fresh oregano (optional) |

1. Combine first 4 ingredients in a small bowl; set aside.

2. Thread mushrooms and next 5 ingredients alternately onto 8 (8-inch) skewers. Brush kabobs with soy sauce mixture.

3. Place kabobs on a baking sheet coated with cooking spray. Broil 3 inches from heat (with electric oven door partially opened) 4 to 5 minutes, basting often with remaining soy sauce mixture.

4. Combine rice and chopped oregano; spoon ½ cup rice on each of 4 individual plates, and place 2 kabobs on each serving. Garnish plates with oregano sprigs, if desired. Yield: 4 servings (2 kabobs and ½ cup rice per serving).

# Peppers Braised with Herbs (photo, page 117)

**Time:** prep 8 minutes; cook 37 minutes

Vegetable cooking spray
| | |
|---|---|
| 1 | teaspoon olive oil |
| 2 | medium onions, thinly sliced |
| ½ | cup dry white wine |
| 2 | medium tomatoes, peeled, seeded, and coarsely chopped |
| 1 | large sweet red pepper, seeded and cut into strips |
| 1 | large green pepper, seeded and cut into strips |
| 1 | large sweet yellow pepper, seeded and cut into strips |
| ¼ | teaspoon salt |
| ½ | cup canned no-salt-added chicken broth, undiluted |
| 9 | fresh mint or basil sprigs, divided |

**1.** Coat a nonstick skillet with cooking spray, and add oil; place over medium-high heat until hot. Add onion, and cook 5 to 7 minutes or until tender, stirring often. Add wine and cook 2 to 3 additional minutes. Stir in tomato, pepper strips, and salt; bring to a boil. Reduce heat to low; cover, and simmer 15 minutes.

**2.** Add broth and 1 mint sprig; cover and simmer 15 minutes. Remove from heat, and allow to cool to room temperature. Remove mint sprig from pepper mixture, and discard. Arrange pepper mixture evenly on 8 individual plates, and garnish with remaining mint sprigs. Yield: 8 servings.

**Each Serving Provides:**

1 Fruit/Vegetable

**Per Serving:**

60 Calories

9.8g Carbohydrate

1.1g Fat (0.2g saturated)

2.4g Fiber

1.5g Protein

0mg Cholesterol

81mg Sodium

18mg Calcium

1.1mg Iron

*tip*

*If you don't have fresh tomatoes, substitute 2 cups of canned no-salt-added plum tomatoes, drained and chopped.*

# Creamy Garlic Mashed Potatoes

**Time:** prep 8 minutes; cook 15 minutes

Each Serving Provides:

1 Bread

Per Serving:

117 Calories

22.9g Carbohydrate

1.4g Fat (0.2g saturated)

1.8g Fiber

4.0g Protein

1mg Cholesterol

242mg Sodium

67mg Calcium

0.9mg Iron

| | |
|---|---|
| 1½ | pounds baking potatoes, peeled and cut into eighths |
| 2 | cloves garlic, peeled |
| ¾ | cup plain nonfat yogurt |
| 1 | tablespoon reduced-calorie margarine |
| ½ | teaspoon salt |
| ⅛ | teaspoon pepper |

**1.** Combine potato and garlic in a medium saucepan; add water to cover. Bring to a boil; reduce heat, cover, and cook 15 minutes or until potato is tender. Drain.

**2.** Add yogurt and remaining ingredients to potato mixture and beat at medium speed of an electric mixer until smooth. Yield: 6 servings.

*tip*

*You can use non-fat sour cream instead of plain nonfat yogurt in this recipe.*

# Oven Hash Browns with Fennel

**Time:** prep 10 minutes; cook 30 minutes

1 medium fennel bulb, cut lengthwise into 1-inch slices
1¼ pounds potatoes, peeled and cubed
1 medium onion, finely chopped
1 tablespoon dried parsley
2 teaspoons vegetable oil
¼ teaspoon salt
⅛ teaspoon freshly ground pepper
Vegetable cooking spray

**1.** Combine fennel slices, potato, and next 5 ingredients in a large bowl; toss gently. Arrange mixture in a single layer on a 15- x 10- x 1-inch jellyroll pan or a roasting pan coated with cooking spray. Bake at 400° for 30 to 35 minutes or until potato is crisp on all sides, stirring occasionally. Serve immediately. Yield: 4 servings.

*Note:* Look for fresh fennel in the produce section of your supermarket. It looks much like celery with its long stalks and feathery top. The bulb base and the stalks can be eaten raw or cooked; the feathery top makes a nice garnish.

**Each Serving Provides:**

1 Bread
1 Fruit/Vegetable
1 Fat

**Per Serving:**

157 Calories
30.4g Carbohydrate
2.8g Fat (0.5g saturated)
3.1g Fiber
4.3g Protein
0mg Cholesterol
160mg Sodium
52mg Calcium
2.2mg Iron

*t i p*

*Slice the celery-like stalks of fennel, and add them to salads for a sweet, delicate anise flavor.*

# Crispy Potato Pancake *(photo, page 118)*

**Time:** prep 10 minutes; cook 25 minutes

| | |
|---|---|
| 1 | (10-ounce) baking potato, peeled and cut into julienne strips |
| ¼ | cup chopped fresh basil |
| 1 | egg white, beaten |
| ¼ | teaspoon salt |
| 1 | clove garlic, minced |

Vegetable cooking spray

| | |
|---|---|
| 3 | tablespoons freshly grated Parmesan cheese |
| ⅛ | teaspoon freshly ground pepper |

**1.** Combine first 5 ingredients in a medium bowl; toss well. Lightly spoon potato mixture into a 9-inch pieplate coated with cooking spray. (Do not press mixture into pieplate.) Sprinkle cheese and pepper evenly over potato mixture. Bake at 400° for 25 to 30 minutes or until crisp; let stand 5 minutes. Cut into 4 wedges. Yield: 4 servings.

## *tip*

*An easy way to chop basil leaves is to pack them in a measuring cup and cut them with kitchen shears.*

# Garlic-Roasted Squash *(photo, pages 60 and 61)*

**Time:** prep 5 minutes; cook 30 minutes

6     medium zucchini, quartered
6     medium-size yellow squash, quartered
1     large Vidalia or other sweet onion, sliced
12    cloves garlic
2     teaspoons olive oil
½    teaspoon salt
¼    teaspoon pepper
Vegetable cooking spray

**1.** Combine first 7 ingredients in a medium bowl; toss well. Arrange squash mixture evenly in a shallow roasting pan coated with cooking spray. Bake at 450° for 30 minutes or until vegetables are tender, stirring every 10 minutes. Yield: 12 servings.

**Each Serving Provides:**
1 Fruit/Vegetable

**Per Serving:**
39 Calories
6.9g Carbohydrate
1.1g Fat (0.2g saturated)
1.8g Fiber
1.8g Protein
0mg Cholesterol
102mg Sodium
32mg Calcium
0.7mg Iron

*tip*

*Preheat the oven while you're preparing the recipe so you won't have to wait to start roasting.*

# Herbed Zucchini Ribbons

**Time:** prep 21 minutes

| | |
|---|---|
| 3 | tablespoons chopped fresh basil |
| ½ | teaspoon grated lemon rind (optional) |
| 3 | tablespoons fresh lemon juice |
| 1 | tablespoon honey |
| 1 | teaspoon vegetable oil |
| ¼ | teaspoon pepper |
| ¼ | teaspoon salt |
| 4 | medium zucchini |
| ¾ | cup finely chopped sweet red pepper |

**1.** Combine first 7 ingredients in a small jar; cover tightly, and shake vigorously to blend. Set aside.

**2.** Slice zucchini lengthwise into thin strips, using a vegetable peeler and applying firm pressure.

**3.** Combine juice mixture, zucchini, and red pepper in a large bowl; toss gently. Serve with a slotted spoon. Yield: 5 servings.

*tip*

*Substitute almost any fresh herb for basil in this recipe; try mint, oregano, or rosemary.*

# Polenta with Parmesan

**Time:** prep 5 minutes; cook 33 minutes

Vegetable cooking spray
1    teaspoon olive oil
1    cup finely chopped onion
2    cups canned low-sodium chicken broth, undiluted
1½  cups water
¼    teaspoon dried crushed red pepper
1¼  cups yellow cornmeal
¼    cup freshly grated Parmesan cheese

**1.** Coat a medium saucepan with cooking spray, and add oil; place over medium-high heat until hot. Add onion, and cook 5 to 7 minutes until onion is tender, stirring often. Add broth, water, and red pepper; bring to a boil.

**2.** Add cornmeal to broth mixture in a slow, steady stream, stirring constantly with a wire whisk. Reduce heat to medium, and simmer 25 to 30 minutes or until mixture pulls away from sides of pan, stirring often. Stir in cheese. Serve immediately. Yield: 6 servings.

*Note:* To make in advance, spoon the cooked polenta into an 8-inch square baking pan and chill. Cut the chilled polenta into 6 slices and bake at 450° for 20 minutes.

**Each Serving Provides:**
2 Bread

**Per Serving:**
152 Calories
25.8g Carbohydrate
3.1g Fat (0.9g saturated)
2.0g Fiber
5.2g Protein
3mg Cholesterol
100mg Sodium
60mg Calcium
1.7mg Iron

*tip*

*Polenta is cooked cornmeal, similar in texture to grits. Try it as an alternative side dish to new or mashed potatoes.*

# Risotto with Peas and Cheese

**Time:** prep 5 minutes; cook 45 minutes

**Each Serving Provides:**

1 Bread

**Per Serving:**

154 Calories

28.0g Carbohydrate

2.2g Fat (0.7g saturated)

1.6g Fiber

5.1g Protein

2mg Cholesterol

93mg Sodium

57mg Calcium

1.9mg Iron

| | |
|---|---|
| 2 | cups canned low-sodium chicken broth, undiluted |
| 2 | cups water |

Vegetable cooking spray

| | |
|---|---|
| 1 | teaspoon olive oil |
| 1 | cup finely chopped onion |
| 1⅓ | cups long-grain rice, uncooked |
| 1 | cup frozen green peas, thawed |
| ¼ | cup freshly grated Parmesan cheese |

**1.** Combine broth and water in a medium saucepan; place over medium heat. Bring to a simmer; reduce heat to low, and keep warm. (Do not boil.)

**2.** Coat a large saucepan with cooking spray, and add oil; place over medium-high heat until hot. Add onion, and cook 5 to 7 minutes or until onion is tender, stirring often. Add rice, and cook, stirring constantly, 2 minutes or until rice is lightly browned. Reduce heat to medium-low.

**3.** Add 1 cup of simmering broth mixture to rice, stirring constantly until most of liquid is absorbed. Add remaining broth, ½ cup at a time, cooking and stirring constantly until each ½ cup addition is absorbed (about 30 minutes). (Rice will be tender and will have a creamy consistency.)

**4.** Add peas, and cook, stirring constantly, until mixture is thoroughly heated. Remove from heat, and stir in cheese. Serve immediately. Yield: 8 servings.

✤ *t i p*

*Risotto is a creamy-textured rice dish created by simmering hot broth and rice. For an extra creamy and more traditional risotto, use high-starch Arborio rice instead of long-grain rice.*

soups

&

sandwiches

# Cold Potato-Cucumber Soup

**Time:** prep: 10 minutes; cook 18 minutes; chill 1 hour

| | |
|---|---|
| 2 | cups canned low-sodium chicken broth, undiluted |
| 2 | (10-ounce) baking potatoes, peeled and cubed |
| | Vegetable cooking spray |
| 1 | medium stalk celery, sliced |
| 1 | shallot, coarsely chopped |
| 1 | medium cucumber, peeled, seeded, and cubed |
| 1 | cup plain nonfat yogurt |
| ¼ | teaspoon salt |
| ⅛ | teaspoon freshly ground pepper |

*tip*

*Use a vegetable peeler to remove the tough strings from celery.*

**1.** Combine broth and potato in a medium saucepan, and bring to a boil. Reduce heat, and simmer 15 minutes or until potato is tender. Remove from heat, and let cool.

**2.** Coat a medium nonstick skillet with cooking spray; place over medium-high heat until hot. Add celery and shallot, and cook 3 minutes or until tender (do not brown), stirring often. Remove from heat; let cool 5 minutes.

**3.** Position knife blade in food processor bowl. Add potato mixture, celery mixture, and cucumber; process until smooth.

**4.** Transfer pureed mixture to a medium bowl; stir in yogurt, salt, and pepper. Cover and chill at least 1 hour. Yield: 4 servings.

# Cauliflower and Leek Soup

**Time:** prep 5 minutes; cook 35 minutes

| | |
|---|---|
| 2 | leeks |
| | Vegetable cooking spray |
| 2 | teaspoons margarine |
| 1 | clove garlic, minced |
| 4 | cups cauliflower flowerets |
| 3 | cups canned low-sodium chicken broth, undiluted |
| 1 | cup evaporated skimmed milk |

**1.** Remove and discard roots and green tops from leeks. Wash thoroughly under running water to remove grit. Cut white portions into thin slices; set aside.

**2.** Coat a medium saucepan with cooking spray, and add margarine; place over medium-high heat until margarine melts. Add leek and garlic, and cook 2 minutes or until leek is tender, stirring often. Add cauliflower and broth; bring to a boil. Reduce heat, cover, and simmer 30 minutes.

**3.** Position knife blade in food processor bowl. Add cauliflower mixture; process until smooth. Return mixture to saucepan. Stir in milk; cook 3 to 4 minutes or until thoroughly heated, stirring occasionally. Yield: 4 servings.

**Each Serving Provides:**

2 Fruit/Vegetable

1 Fat

**Per Serving:**

156 Calories

23.3g Carbohydrate

3.8g Fat (0.8g saturated)

3.2g Fiber

9.6g Protein

3mg Cholesterol

197mg Sodium

246mg Calcium

2.8mg Iron

*tip*

*To clean leeks, split them from top to bottom, and wash them well to remove all dirt.*

# Red Pepper-Tomato Soup *(photo, page 135)*

**Time:** prep 10 minutes; cook 34 minutes

Vegetable cooking spray
1   teaspoon olive oil
1   cup chopped onion
2   cloves garlic, minced
2   medium-size sweet red peppers, chopped
1   (14-ounce) can Italian-style stewed tomatoes, undrained
1   (5-ounce) potato, peeled and chopped (about ⅔ cup)
2   cups canned low-sodium chicken broth, undiluted
2   cups water
Chopped green onions (optional)

**1.** Coat a large saucepan with cooking spray, and add oil; place over medium-high heat until hot. Add onion and garlic, and cook 3 minutes or until tender, stirring often. Add pepper, and cook 3 minutes or until tender, stirring often. Stir in tomato and next 3 ingredients; reduce heat, partially cover, and simmer 25 minutes or until potato is tender. Remove from heat; set aside.

**2.** Position knife blade in food processor bowl. Add vegetable mixture; process until smooth. Return mixture to saucepan, and cook 3 to 4 minutes or until thoroughly heated. Ladle mixture evenly into 8 individual bowls; top with green onions, if desired. Yield: 8 servings.

## tip

*If you don't have a food processor, puree the ingredients for this soup in several batches in the blender.*

# Hearty Vegetable-Beef Soup *(photo, page 136)*

**Time:** prep 12 minutes; cook 32 minutes

1 (14½-ounce) can no-salt-added whole tomatoes, undrained
Vegetable cooking spray
1⅓ cups chopped onion
¾ pound ground round
1 tablespoon all-purpose flour
1 (14¼-ounce) can no-salt-added beef broth, undiluted
1 cup frozen whole-kernel corn
1 cup frozen English peas
2 tablespoons no-salt-added tomato paste
1 teaspoon salt
½ teaspoon dried oregano
½ teaspoon dried marjoram
⅛ teaspoon pepper
⅔ cup elbow macaroni, uncooked

**Each Serving Provides:**

1 Protein/Milk
1 Fruit/Vegetable
80 Optional Calories

**Per Serving:**

193 Calories
24.1g Carbohydrate
2.9g Fat (0.9g saturated)
3.6g Fiber
17.5g Protein
32mg Cholesterol
462mg Sodium
44mg Calcium
2.6mg Iron

**1.** Drain tomatoes, reserving liquid. Coarsely chop tomatoes; set aside tomato and reserved liquid.

**2.** Coat a large saucepan with cooking spray; place over medium-high heat until hot. Add onion and ground round; cook until meat is browned, stirring until it crumbles. Add flour; cook, stirring constantly, 2 minutes. Stir in broth, chopped tomato, and tomato liquid; bring to a boil. Cover, reduce heat, and simmer 15 minutes. Stir in corn and remaining 7 ingredients; bring to a boil. Cover, reduce heat, and simmer 10 minutes or until macaroni is tender. Yield: 6 servings.

# Beef Minestrone

**Time:** prep 10 minutes; cook 52 minutes

Vegetable cooking spray
1      teaspoon olive oil
1      medium onion, finely chopped
1      clove garlic, minced
¼      pound ground round
4      cups canned no-salt-added beef broth, undiluted
1      (5-ounce) potato, peeled and chopped
½      cup finely chopped celery
½      cup finely chopped carrot
½      teaspoon dried basil
½      teaspoon dried oregano
½      teaspoon salt
¼      teaspoon freshly ground pepper
1      (15-ounce) can kidney beans, drained
1      cup shredded green cabbage
⅔      cup elbow macaroni, uncooked
2      tablespoons freshly grated Parmesan cheese

**1.** Coat a large saucepan with cooking spray, and add oil; place over medium-high heat until hot. Add onion and garlic, and cook 5 to 7 minutes or until onion is tender, stirring often. Add ground round, and cook until browned, stirring until it crumbles. Reduce heat; stir in broth and next 7 ingredients. Cover and simmer 30 minutes, stirring occasionally.

**2.** Stir in kidney beans, cabbage, and macaroni; cover and simmer 10 minutes or until macaroni is tender.

**3.** Ladle mixture evenly into 6 soup bowls; top servings evenly with Parmesan cheese. Yield: 6 servings.

*✎ t i p*

*Since you need only 1 cup of shredded cabbage for this recipe, use the already shredded kind in packages in the produce section instead of buying a whole head of cabbage.*

Mango-Kiwi Salsa *(recipe, page 128)*

Apple Strudel *(recipe, page 168)*

# Grilled Cheese *(photo, page 135)*

**Time:** prep 2 minutes; cook 5 minutes

4     (½-inch) slices sourdough bread
1     cup (4 ounces) shredded reduced-fat Cheddar cheese

**1.** Place bread slices on an ungreased baking sheet; broil 5½ inches from heat (with electric oven door partially opened) 2 minutes or until toasted.

**2.** Place bread slices, toasted side down, on baking sheet; sprinkle cheese evenly over bread. Broil 5½ inches from heat (with electric oven door partially opened) 3 to 5 minutes or until cheese melts. Yield: 4 servings (1 open-face sandwich per serving).

**Each Serving Provides:**

1 Protein/Milk
1 Bread

**Per Serving:**

154 Calories
14.1g Carbohydrate
5.9g Fat (3.2g saturated)
0.5g Fiber
11.0g Protein
18mg Cholesterol
365mg Sodium
252mg Calcium
0.8mg Iron

*tip*

*Reduced-fat Cheddar is available only in shredded form. Fat-free Cheddar is sold in slices, but it doesn't melt as well for grilled cheese sandwiches.*

# Greek Chickpea Pitas

**Time:** prep 5 minutes

**Each Serving Provides:**

2 Protein/Milk

1 Bread

**Per Serving:**

358 Calories

55.2g Carbohydrate

8.9g Fat (3.6g saturated)

9.3g Fiber

13.4g Protein

19mg Cholesterol

396mg Sodium

207mg Calcium

4.7mg Iron

| | |
|---|---|
| 1 | (15½-ounce) can chickpeas, drained |
| 1 | small purple onion, sliced |
| 1 | cup cherry tomato halves |
| ¾ | cup (3 ounces) feta cheese, crumbled |
| ½ | cup chopped fresh parsley |
| 2 | tablespoons fresh lemon juice |
| 1 | teaspoon olive oil |
| ¼ | teaspoon freshly ground pepper |
| 4 | (6-inch) pita bread rounds, cut in half |

**1.** Combine all ingredients except pita bread in a medium bowl; spoon mixture evenly into pita halves. Serve immediately. Yield: 4 servings (2 pita halves per serving).

*✎ t i p*

*If you don't have cherry tomatoes on hand, slice a small tomato and cut each slice into fourths.*

# Veggie Burgers *(photo, page 137)*

**Time:** prep 10 minutes; cook 8 minutes

| | |
|---|---|
| 1 | cup instant brown rice, uncooked |
| 1 | small onion, chopped |
| ¼ | pound fresh mushrooms |
| 1 | (15-ounce) can kidney beans, drained |
| 1 | cup shredded carrot |
| 1 | cup (4 ounces) shredded reduced-fat mozzarella cheese |
| ¼ | cup plus 2 tablespoons freshly grated Parmesan cheese |
| 2 | tablespoons tomato paste |
| ¼ | teaspoon salt |
| ⅛ | teaspoon freshly ground pepper |
| 2 | egg whites, lightly beaten |
| Vegetable cooking spray | |
| 4 | lettuce leaves |
| 4 | English muffins, split and toasted |
| 4 | tomato slices |
| 4 | purple onion slices |

**Each Serving Provides:**

2 Protein/Milk
3 Bread
2 Fruit/Vegetable
80 Optional Calories

**Per Serving:**

581 Calories
94.9g Carbohydrate
10.2g Fat (4.7g saturated)
6.3g Fiber
27.8g Protein
22mg Cholesterol
921mg Sodium
445mg Calcium
5.4mg Iron

**1.** Position knife blade in food processor bowl; add first 4 ingredients. Pulse 5 to 7 times or until mixture is finely chopped. Transfer mixture to a large bowl.

**2.** Add carrot and next 6 ingredients to rice mixture, stirring well. Shape mixture into 4 patties.

**3.** Coat grill rack with cooking spray; place on grill over medium-hot coals (350° to 400°). Place patties on rack; grill, covered, 4 to 5 minutes on each side. Place 1 lettuce leaf on the bottom half of each English muffin. Layer 1 patty, 1 tomato slice, and 1 onion slice over each lettuce leaf; top with remaining muffin halves. Yield: 4 servings (1 sandwich per serving).

## ✑ t i p

*Brown rice adds a nutty flavor to the burgers, but you can substitute the same amount of uncooked instant white rice if you don't have brown rice on hand.*

# Lamb Meatball Pitas *(photo, page 138)*

**Time:** prep 15 minutes; chill 1 hour; cook 8 minutes

**Each Serving Provides:**

3 Protein/Milk

2 Bread

**Per Serving:**

378 Calories

39.2g Carbohydrate

8.8g Fat (2.6g saturated)

6.4g Fiber

30.8g Protein

75mg Cholesterol

272mg Sodium

132mg Calcium

5.3mg Iron

Cucumber Raita

| | |
|---|---|
| 1 | pound ground lamb |
| ½ | cup chopped fresh parsley |
| ¼ | cup plus 2 tablespoons soft breadcrumbs |
| 1 | tablespoon chopped fresh mint |
| 2 | teaspoons prepared horseradish |
| 1 | teaspoon prepared mustard |
| 1 | teaspoon dried rosemary |
| 1 | teaspoon Worcestershire sauce |
| ½ | teaspoon freshly ground pepper |
| 2 | cloves garlic, chopped |
| 2 | egg whites, lightly beaten |

Vegetable cooking spray

4    (6-inch) pita bread rounds

Fresh mint sprigs (optional)

**1.** Prepare recipe for Cucumber Raita, allowing at least one hour for sauce to chill.

**2.** Combine lamb, parsley, breadcrumbs, mint, horseradish, mustard, rosemary, Worcestershire sauce, pepper, garlic, and egg whites in a medium bowl; shape mixture into 12 small meatballs.

**3.** Place meatballs in a grill basket coated with cooking spray; place grill basket on rack over medium-hot coals (350° to 400°), and grill, covered, 4 minutes on each side or until meatballs are done.

**4.** Place 3 meatballs on each pita bread round, and top each serving with ¼ cup Cucumber Raita. Garnish each serving with fresh mint sprigs, if desired. Yield: 4 servings (3 meatballs, 1 pita, and ¼ cup raita per serving).

### tip

*Raita (ry-EE-ta), a cooling sauce or relish is especially good to serve with spicy-hot entrées.*

# Cucumber Raita

¾  cup plain nonfat yogurt
2  tablespoons chopped fresh mint
1  tablespoon lemon juice
½  teaspoon freshly ground pepper
¼  teaspoon salt
1  large cucumber, peeled, seeded, and chopped
1  clove garlic, minced

**1.** Combine all ingredients in a bowl; cover and chill at least 1 hour.
Serve as a sauce with lamb, beef, or chicken. Yield: 1 cup.

## 10 Low-Fat Ways to Top a Burger

Set aside plain ol' mustard, mayo, and ketchup. These days the supermarket shelves are groaning with delicious new ways to dress burgers and other sandwiches. Try some of these low-fat ways to add flavor without the fat; dollop them on the meat or spread them over the inside of the bread.

- Creamy reduced-fat salad dressings
- Vegetable salsas (for red meats)
- Fruit salsas (for poultry and fish)
- Fat-free sour cream
- Low-fat yogurt
- Fruit chutneys
- Flavored mustards
- Flavored ketchups
- Barbecue sauce
- Hoisin sauce

# Deluxe Beef Burgers

**Time:** prep 5 minutes; cook 12 minutes

| | |
|---|---|
| 1 | pound ground round |
| ½ | cup chopped green onions |
| ½ | cup shredded carrot |
| ¼ | cup no-salt-added tomato sauce |
| 1 | tablespoon chopped fresh parsley |
| 2 | egg whites, lightly beaten |

Vegetable cooking spray

| | |
|---|---|
| 1 | small onion, sliced and separated into rings |
| 4 | lettuce leaves |
| 4 | tomato slices |
| 4 | hamburger buns, split and toasted |
| 2 | tablespoons ketchup |

**1.** Combine first 6 ingredients in a large bowl; shape mixture into 4 patties. Set aside.

**2.** Coat a large nonstick skillet with cooking spray; place over medium-high heat until hot. Add patties, and cook 5 minutes on each side or until patties are done. Remove patties from skillet; set aside, and keep warm.

**3.** Add onion to skillet, and cook 2 to 3 minutes or until tender, stirring often.

**4.** Place 1 lettuce leaf, 1 tomato slice, and 1 patty on the bottom half of each bun; top patties evenly with cooked onion. Spread ketchup evenly on top halves of buns; place over onion-topped patties. Yield: 4 servings (1 sandwich per serving).

*tip*

*For extra flavor, try using salsa instead of ketchup to top burgers.*

# Curried Chicken Salad Pockets

**Time:** prep 5 minutes

| | |
|---|---|
| 1 | (8-ounce) can pineapple tidbits in juice, drained |
| ½ | cup sliced green onions |
| ½ | cup diced cooked chicken breast (skinned before cooking and cooked without salt or fat) |
| 1 | tablespoon chopped fresh chives |
| 2 | tablespoons reduced-calorie mayonnaise |
| 2 | tablespoons low-fat sour cream |
| 1 | teaspoon curry powder |
| 2 | (6-inch) pita bread rounds, cut in half |

**1.** Combine first 4 ingredients in a medium bowl; set aside. Combine mayonnaise, sour cream, and curry powder; stir into chicken mixture. Spoon mixture evenly into pita halves. Yield: 2 servings (2 pita halves per serving).

**Each Serving Provides:**

1 Protein/Milk

2 Bread

1 Fruit/Vegetable

2 Fat

**Per Serving:**

290 Calories

38.1g Carbohydrate

8.2g Fat (2.4g saturated)

7.3g Fiber

12.9g Protein

35mg Cholesterol

447mg Sodium

96mg Calcium

2.8mg Iron

*tip*

*Keep a can of pineapple tidbits in the refrigerator to make this filling, and you can have a refreshing chilled sandwich in just 5 minutes.*

# Hot Chicken Sandwiches

**Time:** prep 5 minutes; cook 7 minutes

Vegetable cooking spray

1    teaspoon margarine

¼    cup sliced fresh mushrooms

1    teaspoon all-purpose flour

⅓    cup water

½    teaspoon chicken-flavored bouillon granules

¼    cup chopped cooked chicken (skinned before cooking and
      cooked without salt or fat)

2    slices reduced-calorie whole wheat sandwich bread, toasted

**1.** Coat a small skillet with cooking spray, and add margarine; place over medium-high heat until margarine melts. Add mushrooms, and cook 3 to 4 minutes or until tender, stirring often. Sprinkle flour over mushrooms, stirring well. Add water and bouillon granules; cook, stirring constantly, 2 minutes or until mixture is thickened.

**2.** Reduce heat to low; add chicken to mixture, and simmer 2 to 3 minutes or until chicken is thoroughly heated. Spoon chicken mixture evenly over toast slices. Yield: 1 serving (2 open-face sandwiches per serving).

## ✿ *t i p*

*You'll add extra flavor to these sandwiches by using smoked chicken from the deli.*

*desserts*

# Gingered Fruit Cups *(photo, page 42)*

**Time:** prep 5 minutes

**Each Serving Provides:**
1 Fruit/Vegetable
50 Optional Calories

**Per Serving:**
89 Calories
21.4g Carbohydrate
0.3g Fat (0.0g saturated)
3.0g Fiber
1.0g Protein
0.0mg Cholesterol
1mg Sodium
33mg Calcium
0.3mg Iron

| 2 | oranges, peeled and sectioned |
|---|---|
| 1 | (8-ounce) can pineapple chunks in juice, drained |
| 1 | teaspoon peeled, grated gingerroot |
| 4 | sprigs fresh mint (optional) |
| 4 | fortune cookies |

**1.** Combine first 3 ingredients in a small bowl; toss well. Spoon mixture evenly into 4 parfait glasses. Garnish with mint, if desired, and serve with fortune cookies. Yield: 4 servings (1 parfait and 1 fortune cookie per serving).

*✒ t i p*

*To cut pretty orange sections, peel the rind from the orange, then just slide a sharp knife between each side of the sections and the attached membranes.*

# Angel Food Cake & Berries *(photo, page 174)*

**Time:** prep 15 minutes; chill 1 hour

| | |
|---|---|
| 1½ | cups frozen unsweetened raspberries, thawed |
| ¼ | cup orange juice |
| 2 | tablespoons sugar |
| 1 | tablespoon peeled, grated gingerroot |
| 5 | cups fresh strawberries, quartered |
| 3 | cups fresh blueberries |
| 1 | (10-inch) angel food cake |
| 16 | sprigs fresh mint (optional) |

**Each Serving Provides:**

1 Fruit/Vegetable

40 Optional Calories

**Per Serving:**

91 Calories

21.4g Carbohydrate

0.4g Fat (0.0g saturated)

3.5g Fiber

1.7g Protein

0mg Cholesterol

92mg Sodium

27mg Calcium

0.4mg Iron

**1.** Place raspberries in container of an electric blender or food processor; cover and process until smooth, stopping once to scrape down sides. Place pureed raspberries in a wire-mesh strainer; press with back of spoon against strainer to squeeze out juice. Discard seeds remaining in strainer. Return puree to blender; add orange juice and sugar.

**2.** Place gingerroot on an 8-inch cheesecloth square. Bring cheesecloth edges together at top; hold securely. Squeeze cheesecloth bag by hand to extract juice over raspberry mixture in blender; discard grated gingerroot. Pulse to combine raspberry mixture and juice.

**3.** Place strawberries and blueberries in a large bowl; stir in raspberry mixture. Cover and chill at least 1 hour.

**4.** For each serving, place one cake slice on a dessert plate, and top with ½ cup chilled berry mixture; garnish with mint, if desired. Yield: 16 servings.

*tip*

*Any combination of fresh summer berries would be tasty in this recipe.*

# Apple Strudel (*photo, page 156*)

**Time:** prep 10 minutes; cook 36 minutes

| 4 | small Granny Smith apples, peeled, cored, and sliced |
| ¼ | cup water |
| 2 | tablespoons honey |
| ¼ | cup raisins |
| ½ | teaspoon ground cinnamon |
| 6 | sheets frozen phyllo pastry, thawed |
| 3 | tablespoons margarine, melted |
| 1 | tablespoon sugar |
| | Vegetable cooking spray |
| ¾ | cup frozen reduced-calorie whipped topping, thawed |

**1.** Combine first 3 ingredients in a large saucepan; cover and cook over medium heat 6 to 8 minutes or until apple is tender. Remove from heat; stir in raisins and cinnamon. Set aside, and let cool.

**2.** Place 1 phyllo sheet on work surface (keeping remaining phyllo covered); brush evenly with 1½ teaspoons margarine. Top with second phyllo sheet; brush with an additional 1½ teaspoons margarine. Repeat procedure with remaining phyllo sheets and margarine.

**3.** Spoon apple mixture onto 1 corner of phyllo stack; roll up diagonally to enclose filling. Tuck ends under. Make 5 diagonal cuts across top through phyllo with a sharp knife; sprinkle with sugar. Transfer strudel to a baking sheet coated with cooking spray. Bake at 350° for 30 to 35 minutes or until golden.

**4.** Cut strudel into 6 equal slices; top each slice with 2 tablespoons whipped topping. Yield: 6 servings.

## *tip*

*Look for phyllo pastry in the freezer section of your supermarket. For best results, let it thaw in the refrigerator overnight.*

# Banana Pudding

**Time:** prep 10 minutes; cook 32 minutes

½    cup sugar
3    tablespoons cornstarch
⅛    teaspoon salt
2    cups skim milk
1    cup egg substitute
½    teaspoon vanilla extract
28   vanilla wafers
3    medium bananas, peeled and sliced
2    egg whites
¼    teaspoon cream of tartar
3    tablespoons sugar
½    teaspoon vanilla extract

**Each Serving Provides:**

1 Protein/Milk
1 Fruit/Vegetable
140 Optional Calories

**Per Serving:**

227 Calories
42.7g Carbohydrate
3.4g Fat (0.2g saturated)
1.3g Fiber
7.0g Protein
1mg Cholesterol
185mg Sodium
95mg Calcium
1.0mg Iron

**1.** Combine first 3 ingredients in a medium-size heavy saucepan; gradually stir in milk. Cook over medium heat, stirring constantly, until mixture comes to a boil; cook 1 minute, stirring constantly. Remove from heat. Gradually stir about one-fourth of hot milk mixture into egg substitute; add to remaining hot mixture, stirring constantly. Cook over medium heat, stirring constantly, 3 minutes or until thickened. Remove from heat; stir in ½ teaspoon vanilla.

**2.** Arrange half of vanilla wafers in bottom of a 1½-quart casserole; top with half of banana slices and half of custard. Repeat layering procedure with remaining vanilla wafers, banana slices, and custard.

**3.** Beat egg whites and cream of tartar at high speed of an electric mixer until foamy. Gradually add 3 tablespoons sugar, 1 tablespoon at a time, beating until stiff peaks form and sugar dissolves (2 to 4 minutes). Fold in ½ teaspoon vanilla. Spread over custard; seal to edge of dish. Bake at 325° for 25 minutes. Yield: 8 servings.

*tip*

*Reduced-calorie whipped topping makes a quick no-bake alternative to traditional meringue.*

# Peach Crumble *(photo, page 173 and back cover)*

**Time:** prep 5 minutes; cook 25 minutes

2    (16-ounce) cans sliced peaches in light syrup, undrained
Vegetable cooking spray
¾    cup all-purpose flour
3    tablespoons dark brown sugar
¼    cup reduced-calorie stick margarine, chilled
¼    cup frozen reduced-calorie whipped topping, thawed

**1.** Arrange peaches and syrup from can in a 1-quart casserole coated with cooking spray; set aside.

**2.** Combine flour and sugar in a medium bowl; cut in margarine until mixture resembles coarse meal. Sprinkle flour mixture over peaches; bake at 400° for 25 to 35 minutes or until golden.

**3.** Spoon peach mixture evenly into 4 dessert dishes; top each serving with 1 tablespoon whipped topping. Yield: 4 servings.

## tip

*Cut margarine into flour with a pastry blender. Or hold a knife in each hand and pull the knives through the mixture toward each other with blades touching.*

# Mocha Pudding Cake

*m lee 20/20*

**Time:** prep 10 minutes; cook 30 minutes

| | |
|---|---|
| 1 | cup all-purpose flour |
| 2 | teaspoons baking powder |
| ¼ | teaspoon salt |
| 1 | cup sugar, divided |
| ¼ | cup plus 2 tablespoons unsweetened cocoa, divided |
| 1½ | tablespoons instant coffee granules |
| ½ | cup 1% low-fat milk |
| 3 | tablespoons vegetable oil |
| 1 | teaspoon vanilla extract |

Vegetable cooking spray

| | |
|---|---|
| 1 | cup boiling water |
| 1 | cup plus 2 tablespoons low-fat vanilla ice cream |

**1.** Combine flour, baking powder, salt, ⅔ cup sugar, ¼ cup cocoa, and coffee granules in a large bowl; stir well. Combine milk, oil, and vanilla in a small bowl; add to dry ingredients, and stir well. Spoon batter into an 8-inch square pan coated with cooking spray.

**2.** Combine remaining ⅓ cup sugar and 2 tablespoons cocoa. Sprinkle over batter.

**3.** Pour 1 cup boiling water over batter. (Do not stir.) Bake at 350° for 30 minutes or until cake springs back when lightly touched in center. Cut into 9 squares. Serve warm; top with ice cream. Yield: 9 servings (1 cake square and 2 tablespoons ice cream per serving).

**Each Serving Provides:**

1 Bread
1 Fat
80 Optional Calories

**Per Serving:**

226 Calories
39.7g Carbohydrate
6.1g Fat (1.7g saturated)
0.4g Fiber
3.7g Protein
3mg Cholesterol
88mg Sodium
109mg Calcium
1.5mg Iron

*tip*

*You no longer need to sift flour before measuring; just stir the container to break up clumps. It's a good idea to stir cocoa before measuring, too.*

# Chocolate-Drizzled Cream Puffs

Time: prep 20 minutes; cook 35-40 minutes; chill 30 minutes

½   cup water
¼   cup margarine
1    cup all-purpose flour
2    eggs
1    (3.4-ounce) package vanilla instant pudding mix
2    cups skim milk
¼   cup fat-free chocolate syrup

**1.** Combine water and margarine in a medium saucepan over medium-high heat; bring to a boil. Add flour all at once, stirring vigorously until mixture leaves sides of pan and forms a smooth ball. Remove from heat, and let cool 4 to 5 minutes.

**2.** Add eggs, one at a time, beating thoroughly with a wooden spoon after each addition; continue beating until dough is smooth.

**3.** Drop dough in 8 equal mounds 3 inches apart on an ungreased baking sheet. Bake at 400° for 30 to 35 minutes or until golden and puffed. Cool away from drafts. Cut a slit in side of each cream puff; pull out and discard soft dough inside. Set cream puffs aside.

**4.** Prepare pudding according to package directions, using skim milk; transfer pudding to a pastry bag fitted with a plain large round tip. Pipe pudding into cream puffs. Cover and chill filled cream puffs at least 30 minutes.

**5.** Arrange cream puffs on a serving platter; drizzle with chocolate syrup. Yield: 8 servings (1 cream puff per serving).

## ✎ *t i p*

*If you don't have a pastry bag, place the pudding in a heavy-duty, zip-top plastic bag, and seal the top. Clip off one corner of bag, and pipe pudding into cream puffs through this hole.*

Peach Crumble *(recipe, page 170)*

Angel Food Cake & Berries *(recipe, page 167)*

Chocolate Crust Icebox Pie *(recipe, page 181)*

Chocolate Crunch Bars *(recipe, page 187)*

# Fruit and Custard Tart

Time: prep 20 minutes; cook 14 minutes; chill 2 hours

1½   cups all-purpose flour, divided
1½   tablespoons sugar
⅓    cup stick margarine, chilled
1½   tablespoons fresh lemon juice
1½   tablespoons ice water
Vegetable cooking spray
1    (3.4-ounce) package vanilla instant pudding mix
2    cups skim milk
3    medium-size fresh peaches, peeled and sliced
1    cup fresh strawberries, halved
⅓    cup low-sugar apricot spread

**Each Serving Provides:**

1 Bread

1 Fruit/Vegetable

2 Fat

120 Optional Calories

**Per Serving:**

269 Calories

45.0g Carbohydrate

8.1g Fat (1.6g saturated)

1.8g Fiber

5.0g Protein

1mg Cholesterol

205mg Sodium

87mg Calcium

1.2mg Iron

**1.** Set aside 1 tablespoon flour. Place remaining flour and sugar in a large bowl, stirring to combine. Cut in margarine until mixture resembles coarse meal. Sprinkle lemon juice and ice water, 1 tablespoon at a time, over surface of flour mixture; toss with a fork until mixture forms a soft dough. Turn dough out onto work surface sprinkled with reserved 1 tablespoon flour; knead lightly 4 or 5 times. Roll dough into a 10-inch circle. Fit dough into a 9-inch flan dish or pieplate coated with cooking spray; fold edges under, and flute. Prick bottom of pastry with a fork. Bake at 400° for 12 minutes or until lightly browned. Cool completely on a wire rack.

**2.** Prepare pudding mix according to package directions using skim milk; spoon into prepared crust. Arrange peaches and strawberries over pudding.

**3.** Place apricot spread in a small saucepan; place over medium heat until melted. Brush melted apricot spread over peaches and strawberries. Cover and refrigerate at least 2 hours or until thoroughly chilled. Yield: 8 servings.

*tip*

*Dip fresh peaches in boiling water for 15 to 30 seconds, and the skins will slip off easily.*

# Strawberry Cheesecake (photo, page 1)

**Time:** prep 15 minutes; cook 2 hours; chill 8 hours

**Each Serving Provides:**

1 Fat

160 Optional Calories

**Per Serving:**

226 Calories

35.2g Carbohydrate

3.6g Fat (0.6g saturated)

1.5g Fiber

11.8g Protein

12mg Cholesterol

490mg Sodium

215mg Calcium

0.8mg Iron

¼ cup red currant jelly
2 cups fresh strawberries
1¼ cups sugar, divided
Vegetable cooking spray
1 cup graham cracker crumbs
3 tablespoons margarine, melted
½ cup plain low-fat yogurt
2 tablespoons all-purpose flour
4 (8-ounce) packages nonfat cream cheese, softened
¾ cup egg substitute
½ teaspoon grated lemon rind
2 teaspoons fresh lemon juice
1½ teaspoons vanilla extract
14 fresh strawberries, halved
7 kiwifruit slices, halved
14 sprigs fresh mint (optional)

*✍ t i p*

*Cap fresh strawberries after you wash them and their flavor will be more intense.*

**1.** Melt jelly in a saucepan over medium heat, stirring constantly. Remove from heat, and cool slightly. Position knife blade in food processor bowl; add 2 cups strawberries and 2 tablespoons sugar. Process 1 to 2 minutes or until smooth; add to jelly mixture, stirring well. Transfer mixture to a bowl; cover and chill.

**2.** Coat a 9-inch springform pan with cooking spray. Combine graham cracker crumbs, 2 tablespoons sugar, and margarine; stir well. Firmly press crumb mixture evenly into bottom of pan. Set aside.

**3.** Combine yogurt and flour in a large bowl; beat at low speed of an electric mixer until well blended. Add cream cheese; beat at medium speed until smooth. Add remaining 1 cup sugar, egg substitute, lemon rind, lemon juice, and vanilla; beat well. Spoon over crumb mixture.

**4.** Bake at 300° for 1 hour (center will be soft but will firm when chilled). Turn off oven, and partially open oven door; leave cheesecake in oven 1 hour. Remove from oven, and let cool to room temperature on a wire rack. Cover and chill 8 hours.

**5.** Spoon 2 tablespoons strawberry mixture onto each dessert plate. Arrange cheesecake slices over strawberry mixture. Garnish each slice with 2 strawberry halves and a kiwifruit slice. Garnish with mint, if desired. Yield: 14 servings.

## *Curing Cheesecake Cracks*

Cheesecakes crack. It's just a fact of life. But there are a few techniques you can use to lessen the chance of a crater (and your embarrassment) the next time you bake a cheesecake. Try these tips from our Test Kitchens:

• Don't overbeat the Neufchâtel or cream cheese mixture. The more air you whip into the mixture, the more likely it is that the cheesecake will crack as it cools.

• Bake cheesecake at a low oven temperature-about 300° or 325°. The low temperature allows the filling to heat and cook slowly.

• Turn off the oven after the cheesecake bakes. (You'll know it's done when the cake is set around the edges, but the center still wiggles a bit when you shake the pan slightly. If you bake the cake until it is completely set,

it will be too dry.) Let the cheesecake cool slowly as the oven cools to avoid an abrupt change in temperature which can cause cracking. Then allow it to cool at room temperature before you place it in the refrigerator.

• If your cheesecake still develops an unattractive crack, top it with fresh fruit slices, a sauce, or even melted jelly (red current jelly is especially good over plain cheesecake). Or cut the cheesecake slices in the kitchen, rather than presenting the whole cake at the table; your guests will never suspect a thing.

# Marble Sour Cream Cheesecake

**Time:** prep 15 minutes; cook 1 hour and 55 minutes; chill 8 hours

Each Serving Provides:

210 Optional Calories

Per Serving:

223 Calories

17.2g Carbohydrate

12.4g Fat (6.6g saturated)

0.0g Fiber

9.3g Protein

108mg Cholesterol

229mg Sodium

47mg Calcium

0.7mg Iron

Vegetable cooking spray

| | |
|---|---|
| 8 | chocolate wafer cookies, crushed |
| 2 | (8-ounce) packages Neufchâtel cheese, softened |
| 2 | cups nonfat sour cream |
| ½ | cup sugar |
| 4 | eggs |
| 1 | teaspoon almond extract |
| ½ | teaspoon vanilla extract |
| 2 | tablespoons unsweetened cocoa |

**1.** Coat a 9-inch springform pan with cooking spray; wrap a large piece of heavy-duty aluminum foil around bottom and up sides of springform pan. Sprinkle cookie crumbs in bottom of pan; set aside.

**2.** Beat Neufchâtel cheese and sour cream at medium speed of an electric mixer until creamy. Gradually add sugar, beating well. Add eggs, one at a time, beating at low speed after each addition. Stir in almond and vanilla extracts.

**3.** Spoon 2 cups of batter into a medium bowl; add cocoa, stirring well. Pour half of chocolate batter into prepared pan. Spoon plain batter over chocolate batter. Drop remaining chocolate batter, one tablespoon at a time, over plain batter. Swirl with a knife to create a marbled effect.

**4.** Place prepared springform pan in a shallow pan. Add hot water to pan to depth of 1 inch. Bake at 325° for 55 minutes (center will be soft but will firm when chilled). Turn off oven, and partially open oven door; leave cheesecake in oven 1 hour. Remove from oven, and let cool to room temperature on a wire rack. Cover and chill 8 hours. Yield: 12 servings.

## tip

*To soften Neufchâtel or cream cheese quickly, place two unwrapped 8-ounce packages in a medium bowl, and microwave at HIGH for 1 to 1¼ minutes.*

# Chocolate Crust Icebox Pie (photo, page 175)

**Time:** prep 5 minutes; cook 10 minutes; freeze 2 hours

¼ cup sugar
2 tablespoons margarine
1¼ cups chocolate graham cracker crumbs
Vegetable cooking spray
4 cups vanilla nonfat frozen yogurt, softened
2 tablespoons chopped walnuts
2 tablespoons fat-free chocolate syrup
12 fresh raspberries (optional)

**1.** Position knife blade in food processor bowl. Combine sugar and margarine in processor bowl; add graham cracker crumbs, and pulse until well blended.

**2.** Firmly press crumb mixture evenly over bottom and up sides of a 9-inch pieplate coated with cooking spray. Bake at 350° for 10 minutes. Set aside, and cool completely.

**3.** Spoon yogurt into prepared crust, and sprinkle with walnuts. Drizzle with chocolate syrup. Cover and freeze at least 2 hours. Garnish with raspberries, if desired. Yield: 8 servings.

**Each Serving Provides:**

1 Bread
1 Fat
110 Optional Calories

**Per Serving:**

230 Calories
40.2g Carbohydrate
6.1g Fat (0.7g saturated)
0.7g Fiber
5.3g Protein
0mg Cholesterol
196mg Sodium
141mg Calcium
0.8mg Iron

### tip

*It will take about 20 chocolate graham cracker squares to equal 1¼ cups of crumbs.*

# Orange-Lemon Sorbet

**Time:** prep 10 minutes; cook 1 minute; freeze 8 hours

Zest of 3 small oranges
Zest of 3 lemons
1 tablespoon finely chopped fresh mint
½ cup hot water
¾ cup cold water
¼ cup sugar
¾ cup fresh orange juice ✓
½ cup fresh lemon juice ✓

**1.** Combine first 4 ingredients in a small bowl; set aside to cool. Strain, discarding zest and mint; reserve flavored water.

**2.** Combine ¾ cup water and sugar; cook over medium heat, stirring constantly, until sugar dissolves. Let cool. Combine flavored water, sugar syrup, orange juice, and lemon juice. Pour mixture into an 8-inch square pan; freeze 8 hours or until firm.

**3.** Spoon frozen mixture into container of an electric blender or food processor; cover and process until smooth. Serve immediately, or cover and freeze until ready to serve. Yield: 6 servings.

### ✿ t i p

*You'll get about ¼ cup of juice from an orange, and about 3 tablespoons of juice from a lemon.*

# Black and White Sodas

**Time:** prep 5 minutes

| | |
|---|---|
| 2 | cups skim milk |
| 3 | tablespoons chocolate syrup |
| 2 | cups nonfat vanilla ice cream |
| 2 | cups nonfat chocolate ice cream |
| 1 | cup club soda |
| ¼ | cup frozen reduced-calorie whipped topping, thawed |
| 4 | maraschino cherries |

**1.** Combine milk and syrup; stir well. Pour evenly into 4 large soda glasses. Place ½ cup vanilla ice cream and ½ cup chocolate ice cream in each glass; add ¼ cup club soda to each glass. Top each with 1 tablespoon whipped topping and 1 cherry. Yield: 4 servings.

**Each Serving Provides:**

180 Optional Calories

**Per Serving:**

197 Calories

38.8g Carbohydrate

1.1g Fat (0.7g saturated)

0.3g Fiber

6.9g Protein

3mg Cholesterol

136mg Sodium

161mg Calcium

0.3mg Iron

*tip*

*If you don't have club soda on hand, use ginger ale instead.*

# Swiss Coffee Cream

**Time:** prep 5 minutes; cook 1 minute; chill 1 hour

| | |
|---|---|
| 1 | envelope unflavored gelatin |
| ¼ | cup water |
| 1 | cup evaporated skimmed milk, chilled |
| 1 | cup part-skim ricotta cheese |
| ⅔ | cup instant nonfat dry milk powder |
| 2 | teaspoons sugar |
| 1 | teaspoon instant coffee granules |
| ½ | cup frozen reduced-calorie whipped topping, thawed |

Ground cinnamon

*tip*

*Look for cartons of ricotta cheese in the dairy case near where you'll find cottage cheese.*

**1.** Sprinkle gelatin over water in a small saucepan; let stand 1 minute to soften. Place over low heat and cook, stirring until gelatin dissolves. Set gelatin mixture aside.

**2.** Pour evaporated milk into container of an electric blender or food processor; cover and process until thick and creamy. Add ricotta cheese, milk powder, sugar, and coffee granules; process until combined. Add dissolved gelatin; process just until combined.

**3.** Pour mixture evenly into 4 parfait glasses; cover and chill at least 1 hour or until set.

**4.** Top each serving with 2 tablespoons whipped topping; sprinkle each with cinnamon. Yield: 4 servings.

# Almond Crescents

**Time:** prep 15 minutes; chill 1 hour; cook 20 minutes

2     cups all-purpose flour
¼     cup ground almonds
⅛     teaspoon salt
⅔     cup reduced-calorie margarine, softened
⅓     cup powdered sugar, divided
½     cup egg substitute
1     teaspoon vanilla extract
Vegetable cooking spray

**1.** Combine first 3 ingredients in a large bowl. Add margarine, ¼ cup sugar, egg substitute, and vanilla; stir until well blended (mixture will be stiff). Knead lightly until smooth. Shape dough into a ball; wrap in wax paper, and chill 1 hour.

**2.** Shape dough into 1-inch balls; roll each into a log, and shape into a crescent. Place on baking sheets coated with cooking spray. Bake at 325° for 10 to 15 minutes. Remove to wire racks to cool slightly; sprinkle cookies with remaining 1 tablespoon plus 1 teaspoon powdered sugar, and cool completely on wire racks. Yield: 40 cookies (1 per serving).

**Each Serving Provides:**

1 Fat

**Per Serving:**

53 Calories

6.0g Carbohydrate

2.8g Fat (0.3g saturated)

0.4g Fiber

1.3g Protein

0mg Cholesterol

41mg Sodium

5mg Calcium

0.4mg Iron

*tip*

*For most baked products, it's best to use stick margarine rather than the spread or squeeze types.*

# Ginger Cookies

**Time:** prep 8 minutes; cook 16 minutes

¼    cup margarine
¼    cup firmly packed brown sugar
3    tablespoons honey
¾    cup all-purpose flour
2    teaspoons ground ginger
⅛    teaspoon salt
Vegetable cooking spray

**1.** Combine first 3 ingredients in a medium saucepan; place over low heat, and cook, stirring constantly, until margarine melts.

**2.** Combine flour, ginger, and salt in a medium bowl; add margarine mixture, stirring well.

**3.** Drop dough by rounded teaspoonfuls onto a large baking sheet coated with cooking spray. Bake at 400° for 15 to 20 minutes or until lightly browned. Transfer to wire racks; cool completely. Yield: 16 cookies (1 per serving).

*✎ t i p*

*Cookies can be tough if you use too much flour. Lightly spoon flour into the measuring cup; never pack it.*

# Chocolate Crunch Bars *(photo, page 176)*

**Time:** prep 5 minutes; cook 5 minutes

Vegetable cooking spray
6    cups cocoa crisp rice cereal
1½  tablespoons margarine
½   (16-ounce) package miniature marshmallows
1½  tablespoons reduced-fat creamy peanut butter
⅓   cup reduced-fat semisweet chocolate morsels

**1.** Spray a large bowl with cooking spray; place rice cereal in bowl. Set aside.

**2.** Combine margarine and marshmallows in a medium saucepan; cook over medium-low heat, stirring constantly, until marshmallows melt and mixture is smooth. Stir in peanut butter.

**3.** Pour marshmallow mixture over cereal, stirring until cereal is well coated using a rubber spatula coated with cooking spray. Stir in chocolate morsels. Press mixture into a 13- x 9- x 2-inch pan coated with cooking spray. Let cool completely. Cut into 24 bars. Yield: 2 dozen (1 bar per serving).

**Each Serving Provides:**
70 Optional Calories

**Per Serving:**
96 Calories
19.0g Carbohydrate
2.2g Fat (1.1g saturated)
0.0g Fiber
1.1g Protein
0mg Cholesterol
90mg Sodium
1mg Calcium
0.0mg Iron

### *tip*

*Coat your hands with cooking spray before pressing the sticky mixture into the pan, and the cereal won't stick to your hands.*

# Low-Fat Ingredient Substitutions

| Needed ingredient | Substitute |
|---|---|
| **Fats and Oils:** | |
| Butter and/or margarine | Reduced-calorie margarine or margarine made with safflower, soybean, corn, canola, or peanut oil; reduced-calorie stick margarine in baked products |
| Mayonnaise | Nonfat or reduced-calorie mayonnaise |
| Oil | Safflower, soybean, corn, canola, or peanut oil in reduced amount |
| Salad dressing | Nonfat or oil-free dressing |
| Shortening | Soybean, corn, canola, or peanut oil in amount reduced by one-third |
| **Dairy Products:** | |
| Sour cream | Low-fat or nonfat sour cream; low-fat or nonfat yogurt |
| Whipping cream | Chilled evaporated skimmed milk, whipped |
| American, Cheddar, colby, Edam, Swiss | Cheeses with 5 grams of fat or less per ounce such as reduced-fat and part-skim cheeses |
| Cottage cheese | Nonfat or 1% low-fat cottage cheese |
| Cream cheese | Nonfat or light process cream cheese; Neufchâtel cheese |
| Ricotta cheese | Nonfat, lite, or part-skim ricotta cheese |
| Milk, whole or 2% | Skim milk; ½% milk; 1% milk |
| Ice cream | Nonfat or low-fat frozen yogurt; nonfat or low-fat ice cream; sherbet; sorbet |
| **Meats, Poultry, and Eggs:** | |
| Bacon | Canadian bacon; turkey bacon; lean ham |
| Beef, veal, lamb, pork | Chicken, turkey, or lean cuts of meat trimmed of all visible fat |
| Ground beef | Extra-lean or ultra-lean ground beef; ground turkey |
| Luncheon meat | Skinned, sliced turkey or chicken breast; lean ham; lean roast beef |
| Poultry | Skinned poultry |
| Tuna packed in oil | Tuna packed in water |
| Turkey, self basting | Turkey basted with fat-free broth |
| Egg, whole | 2 egg whites or ¼ cup egg substitute |
| **Miscellaneous:** | |
| Chocolate, unsweetened | 3 tablespoons unsweetened cocoa plus 1 tablespoon margarine per ounce of chocolate |
| Fudge sauce | Fat-free fudge sauce or chocolate syrup |
| Nuts | One-third to one-half less, toasted |
| Soups, canned | 99% fat-free or reduced-sodium condensed cream soups |

# Metric Equivalents

The recipes that appear in this cookbook use the standard United States method for measuring liquid and dry or solid ingredients (teaspoons, tablespoons, and cups). The information in the following charts is provided to help cooks outside the U.S. successfully use these recipes. All equivalents are approximate.

## Metric Equivalents for Different Types of Ingredients

A standard cup measure of a dry or solid ingredient will vary in weight depending on the type of ingredient. A standard cup of liquid is the same volume for any type of liquid. Use the following chart when converting standard cup measures to grams (weight) or milliliters (volume).

| Standard Cup | Fine Powder (ex. flour) | Grain (ex. rice) | Granular (ex. sugar) | Liquid Solids (ex. butter) | Liquid (ex. milk) |
|---|---|---|---|---|---|
| 1 | 140 g | 150 g | 190 g | 200 g | 240 ml |
| ¾ | 105 g | 113 g | 143 g | 150 g | 180 ml |
| ⅔ | 93 g | 100 g | 125 g | 133 g | 160 ml |
| ½ | 70 g | 75 g | 95 g | 100 g | 120 ml |
| ⅓ | 47 g | 50 g | 63 g | 67 g | 80 ml |
| ¼ | 35 g | 38 g | 48 g | 50 g | 60 ml |
| ⅛ | 18 g | 19 g | 24 g | 25 g | 30 ml |

## Useful Equivalents for Dry Ingredients by Weight

(To convert ounces to grams, multiply the number of ounces by 30)

| | | | | |
|---|---|---|---|---|
| 1 oz | = | 1/16 lb | = | 30 g |
| 4 oz | = | ¼ lb | = | 120 g |
| 8 oz | = | ½ lb | = | 240 g |
| 12 oz | = | ¾ lb | = | 360 g |
| 16 oz | = | 1 lb | = | 480 g |

## Useful Equivalents for Length

(To convert inches to centimeters, multiply the number of inches by 2.5)

| | | | | | | |
|---|---|---|---|---|---|---|
| 1 in | = | | | = | 2.5 cm | |
| 6 in | = | ½ ft | | = | 15 cm | |
| 12 in | = | 1 ft | | = | 30 cm | |
| 36 in | = | 3 ft | = 1 yd | = | 90 cm | |
| 40 in | = | | | = | 100 cm | = 1 m |

## Useful Equivalents for Liquid Ingredients by Volume

| | | | | |
|---|---|---|---|---|
| ¼ tsp | | | | 1 ml |
| ½ tsp | | | | 2 ml |
| 1 tsp | | | | 5 ml |
| 3 tsp | = 1 tbls | | = ½ fl oz | = 15 ml |
| | 2 tbls | = ⅛ cup | = 1 fl oz | = 30 ml |
| | 4 tbls | = ¼ cup | = 2 fl oz | = 60 ml |
| | 5⅓ tbls | = ⅓ cup | = 3 fl oz | = 80 ml |
| | 8 tbls | = ½ cup | = 4 fl oz | = 120 ml |
| | 10⅔ tbls | = ⅔ cup | = 5 fl oz | = 160 ml |
| | 12 tbls | = ¾ cup | = 6 fl oz | = 180 ml |
| | 16 tbls | = 1 cup | = 8 fl oz | = 240 ml |
| | 1 pt | = 2 cups | = 16 fl oz | = 480 ml |
| | 1 qt | = 4 cups | = 32 fl oz | = 960 ml |
| | | | 33 fl oz | = 1000 ml = 1 l |

## Useful Equivalents for Cooking/Oven Temperatures

| | Fahrenheit | Celsius | Gas Mark |
|---|---|---|---|
| Freeze Water | 32° F | 0° C | |
| Room Temperature | 68° F | 20° C | |
| Boil Water | 212° F | 100° C | |
| Bake | 325° F | 160° C | 3 |
| | 350° F | 180° C | 4 |
| | 375° F | 190° C | 5 |
| | 400° F | 200° C | 6 |
| | 425° F | 220° C | 7 |
| | 450° F | 230° C | 8 |
| Broil | | | Grill |

# Recipe Index